DYING TO LEAD:
SACRIFICIAL LEADERSHIP
IN A SELF-CENTERED WORLD

By

Robert McKenna, Ph.D.

Dying To Lead:
Sacrificial Leadership In A Self-Centered World
by Robert McKenna, Ph.D.

Printed in the United States of America

ISBN 978-1-60647-684-0

www.xulonpress.com

This book is dedicated to my Dad. He is a man who calculates the cost of leading, understanding what's at stake, and still chooses to lead each day of his life for the sake of his followers, and most importantly, for his God.

Praises for Dying to Lead

"Every Christian who is in a position of leadership needs to read this book! Rob McKenna is a stellar researcher who has the unusual knack of being able to communicate his findings in ways that are not only understandable, but engaging and motivating. In my opinion, you run the risk of being dead in the water if you don't read *Dying to Lead*."

-Les Parrott, Ph.D., Founder
of RealRelationships.com and
Author of *Trading Places*

"The heart felt cry of every Christian leader I know is to somehow move their organization to a level of excellence on a scale that can only be measured in a kingdom scale and economy. Rob McKenna's work provides important language and thinking which advances leadership in new and important ways."

-Steven G.W. Moore, Executive
Director, The M.J. Murdock
Charitable Trust

"In *Dying to Lead*, Dr. McKenna has woven together the unique characteristics of truly inspirational leadership. In a day when it has been all about me, he shows us that sacrificial leadership is a key ingredient to answering the universal questions of meaning, faith, purpose in the context of community."

-Alfred Lopus, President, Best Christian Workplaces Institute

"Dying to Lead gives us an authentic peek into the heart of a leader revealing stuff that most leaders are encouraged not to discuss. Questions ranging from "Why do I really lead?" to "Do I have the courage to be irrelevant?" to "How can I lead when I'm such a dork?" will stretch your thinking about your leadership and you will have no choice but to grow."

-Jim Lange, Author, *Bleedership*,

"Rob McKenna has taken an intriguing approach to helping leaders of all levels assess their capabilities and motives. It is a challenging book, in that it asks questions that require some reflection and more than a cursory read. The book has been structured in a way that encourages thoughtful consideration of each chapter and is ideally suited to guide discussions with a mentor or small group. If you're a leader looking for more than an organizational gimmick or trick to improve your leadership ability, take the time to *read and think* through *Dying to Lead*. You'll finish with a better understanding and appreciation of why you are leading."

-Mike Kilbane, Managing
Director, OptiSource Partners

"I'll say right now that I was deeply moved from reading *Dying to Lead*, and that I've never read anything quite like it. It is written from the heart, and is both challenging to managers and practical at the same time. Most importantly, it got right to the issue of character and spiritual values and how we need to <u>die to self</u> while moving forward and becoming an instrument of God. *Dying to Lead* is an important book for managers."

-Susan Arnold, Manager,
Starbucks Coffee Company

Table of Contents

Part I 19
The Question of Purpose: Why Do You Lead?

Foreword xi
Chapter 1: What Is a Leader? 21
Chapter 2: Three Questions Down 27
Chapter 3: Whose Are You? 33
Chapter 4: Dying to Lead 43
Chapter 5: The Relative Unimportance of Results 49
Chapter 6: Is God Showing Up? 53
Chapter 7: Don't Let the Gift Go to Your Head 59
Chapter 8: Successful Leaders Have Much to Carry 65

Part II 71
The Question of Identity: Whose Are You?

Chapter 9: Reluctance to Lead 73
Chapter 10: The Courage to Be Irrelevant 79
Chapter 11: Steadfast 83
Chapter 12: Who Are You, Really? 87
Chapter 13: The Right Stuff 93
Chapter 14: Leaders Are Dorks 101

Part III **107**
The Question of Perspective: How Do You See It?

Chapter 15: You Do Have a Choice 109
Chapter 16: What's That to You? 113
Chapter 17: Embrace Your Inner Nobody.......................119
Chapter 18: Thank God He's Not Fair.............................125
Chapter 19: Who Made This Day Possible? 129
Chapter 20: Fear, Grace, and the Unlikely Leader...........133

Part IV..**139**
The Question of Action: What You Must Do?

Chapter 21: Who Will Lead Next? 141
Chapter 22: Communicating Hope 147
Chapter 23: Whatever It Takes...153
Chapter 24: Shut Up! 159
Chapter 25: Throwing Yourself Under the Bus 165
Chapter 26: Looking for Character? 171
Chapter 27: Givers and Takers...177
Chapter 28: What Do You Want?......................................181
Chapter 29: Reclaiming Vocation 187
Chapter 30: Puking 193
Chapter 31: Dying to Lead Characterisitics.....................199

Foreword

Many of us who were dying to lead when we started had a very limited concept of how much we would have to sacrifice, and even less awareness of how leadership success would cause us to lose sight of our early inspirations. Success gives you things. It builds powerful expectations in others about us that often translate into expectations we have for ourselves. Success gives you the power to get more resources, more relationships, and to raise your expectations for your future success. The problem with having more is that it naturally fuels the desire to protect what you have accumulated, psychologically, physically, emotionally, and relationally. Having more to protect often takes us further and further away from the calling that we originally heard when we dreamed of what we would become, leading for the sake of obedience to God and to others, and being willing to sacrifice whatever is necessary for the good of those we lead.

But, interestingly enough, success isn't the only thing that can make us focus on ourselves. Failure can create an equal or greater pressure on you as a leader to buckle down and think of number one. Consider the last time you experienced a serious failure, a leadership setback, or personal pain and suffering of some kind. Failure causes most of us to move into a self-preservation mode in order to shelter ourselves and those we love from even more failure or pain.

Whether you find yourself in a season of success or failure as a leader, the underlying assumption of this book is that your leading matters, and that most of the wrong turns taken by leaders and organizations come down to one thing: the fact that when you are dying to lead, your first step will be to consider the selfish parts of you that may need to die before you go and lead, and that process has to be repeated every day you lead.

What Is Leadership?

We talk about leadership so much that sometimes we forget why we started talking in the first place. Leadership has become a frustrating topic. We forget that leading others is about leading *others*, and that leading others is just plain hard. So let's get some things straight. When we talk about leadership development, leadership, or leading, we're mostly talking about people who will be responsible for the work, development, motivation, direction, and perceptions of others. We're looking for people who will step up to the plate and start leading other people. Now, in the spirit of honesty, many of the people who pick up the mantle of leadership want it in part because they like power, influence, and autonomy. For others, it's about being or doing something significant. Whatever the case, you are leading others somewhere.

Therefore, if you're in a formal or informal position of leadership—a manager, executive, pastor, parent, or volunteer leader—I need to remind you of three things. First, most likely you chose to be in a position of leadership. Even if you were asked to lead something or someone, you could have said no. While that may be a stretch for parents, you could have put your kid up for adoption (a bit of a stretch, I know, but nevertheless a choice you could have made). You made the choice. Second, if you are in a position of leadership, at some level you are responsible for the work of others, and their work will somehow be related to the value and quality of your work. Third, you are responsible for the development of those you lead, and you chose that responsibility. This is the most exciting and challenging news of all.

Over and over again in this book you will hear that leading is about knowing why you lead, for the sake of what or whom you lead, and about the fact that leadership implies the leading of others. Many leaders are very interested in the "how" questions. How do I get from point A to point B? How do I grow my organization? How do I lead more effectively? These questions are important, relevant to our personal and organizational success, provide us with stepping stones to get us moving forward, and motivate us to get out of bed in the morning. However, the questions that answer "how" provide little or no direction or purpose to our movement. It's often said that the only consistency in today's organizations is change. That statement, while it highlights the tremendous amount we're doing and changing every day, says very little about the purpose of our movements. The foundational questions for leaders must start long before we are looking into the "how to" answers to questions. We have to begin with the questions of "why." I'm not talking about the "why" questions we ask about others. Why did he do that? Why is my organization downsizing? Why in the world did my CEO make that statement? The important "why" questions focus on your purpose, the direction you will take, and for whom or what you will take your next step.

Answering the question of why with all honesty is good for us as leaders because it surfaces all the insecurities that cause us to project something we're not. It also gathers the right people around you for the right reasons because what they see is the real you trying to figure out your purpose as it relates to them. "Why" is dangerous because it also surfaces a lot of shame in leaders who have never asked the question. But moving from shame to an honest answer is critical because your followers will see the real you and be able to make their own honest choices in following you. For that reason, "why" is important because it always brings us back to why we were crazy enough to lead in the first place. It provides us with so much more than a way to get up in the morning and lead—it gives us the reason we get up and lead.

What Do We Know About Leading?

Leadership theory has come a long way. If you are a leader, you are probably aware of the abundance of leadership models out there. In the last century alone, and since the dawn of the industrial age, we have seen a logical progression in how we look at leadership and the most common suggestions for leaders. We continue to see ideas for how to make you more effective as a leader, for the sake of the business, or for the sake of yourself. We also see suggestions for how to behave as a leader, the difference between leading and managing, and how to lead in different contexts (individuals, teams, organizations, cultures). We have also witnessed the emergence of leadership intelligence, personality, and now, more recently, emotional intelligence as predictors of leadership effectiveness.

Due to a backlash against ethical violations in business, we have also seen an emergence of character as the focus of leadership, and more specifically the topic of humility. This backlash has given birth to the challenge of defining character, interviewing for character in leaders, and understanding how character is presented by leaders. Finally, in the last decade in Western business culture, we have witnessed an awakened focus on service, giving back, and philanthropic behaviors in leaders. All these ways of approaching leading have given us much to discuss at the water cooler, a full docket of things to complain about in our leaders, and a great deal of insight into the actual job of leading.

While all these ways of portraying, modeling, and improving leadership have taught us much, for the sake of moving forward, I now need you to reflect briefly on all these leadership approaches. Reflect just long enough to think about your own mental models of how leadership works, and then put them all aside. Don't put them aside because they don't matter, but put them aside long enough to consider leading on a level that may or may not make sense in your current way of thinking.

This book is offering a different perspective on leadership for the leader slugging it out day by day in the trenches, feeling a calling to something more, and hoping and trying to make a difference. As you reflect on the pages to come, you will notice that this book is based on many leadership examples and principles from the Bible. More specifically, the idea of sacrificial leadership proposed here is based on the person of Jesus Christ as the Son of God, as God incarnate who came as a human being to earth, and as a model for the necessity of leadership sacrifice. This is a deliberate and necessary assumption behind the following chapters because the Bible is full of leaders who were normal people just like you and me, but people who were constantly faced with the dilemma of making their leadership about themselves—their own needs and wants— as opposed to God's needs and wants for them. It's certainly not necessary for you to be a Christian to understand the concept of sacrifice, but it is important to understand the context within which sacrificial leadership is being proposed as another way to look at leading.

The key question for you as a leader is this. If you took the chance to believe that God loves you just the way you are, that He sacrificed all for you through His Son's death on the cross, that your every breath mattered to Him, and that He is present with you in every moment of your life, what would you do differently today? How would that impact what you do and who you are in the next moment? It's tough for many leaders to consider sacrifice when they are surrounded by the personal and organizational pressure to succeed, but God's sacrifice through the death of His Son provides a different model by which we can live our lives.

It's my hope that this book will challenge you as much as it encourages and provokes you. I purposely intend to fail on a number of fronts. I will fail to provide you with another "how to" book on leadership, but instead may cause you to think about leadership in a different way. In this process, I'll fail to define God's terms completely for you. I will, however, ask you to consider the places in your leading where you get in your own way, the things inside of you that cause you to lead on your terms and according to your agenda alone. The fact is that as soon as you step into the formal or informal role of leader, everything changes and some new questions come into play. How does my need to be courageous and purposeful work with my need for humility? How do I stay connected to those I'm leading while also staying true to what I want? How do I maintain faith when I also know I have doubts? Is it okay to have my own plans when I'm supposed to surrender my life to God's plan? How can I be a godly person at work when I feel like I don't have a choice about putting my business's or my family's success first and foremost in my work life? These are all normal questions for people. I know because those around me ask them all the time, and I see these challenges in my own life.

This book is written for the leader with little time to read. For this reason, the chapters are short and followed by reflection questions you can discuss with other leaders like you. It is my hope that you may take a few minutes each day or each week to reflect on your faith in relationship to your leadership, and your leadership in relationship to your followers, and most importantly to God. At the center of the book are three questions you'll hear me ask you in a variety of ways. First, who are you leading? Second, who do you need to lead? And, third, what would you sacrifice for that privilege? Whether you call yourself a follower of Jesus Christ or not, it is my hope that this book will challenge you and provide you with renewed insights into your own faith, calling, and leadership.

Part I

The Question of Purpose: Why Do You Lead?

Chapter 1

What Is a Leader?

Follower:	Hey leader, what does your title mean? Your signature line in your emails to me says "leader." I'm not sure what that means.
Leader:	That's a good question. It means I got promoted. It also means that someone looked at me and said, "Now that's a leader!" I hope that helps.
Follower:	So leader means that someone saw you as a leader and gave you a promotion. I watch some of the things you do, and someone told me that your role somehow relates to mine, but I'm not sure how. Last year you sat next to me, and now you sit by Bob. He's a leader too, right? What does he do? I'm still very confused about your title. Can you start over and tell me as if I were five years old because I still don't get it?
Leader:	You don't get it because you aren't a leader yet. Maybe someday you'll understand. For now just know that I'm successful, I'm

making more money, I have the right stuff, the personality, and I do all the right things. I read lots of books about leadership as well. One book said that leaders aren't managers and another said that leadership is learned. This other one said I was born with it. Another one with cartoons about a weird-looking little fellow made fun of leadership. It's from the newspaper. Come to think of it, I actually read those cartoons before I became a leader and enjoyed them a lot. I don't think they're funny anymore. Anyway, I'll give you a pile of those books if you ever become a leader.

Follower: Thanks. I think I'm beginning to get it. You are successful, you have the right stuff, you talk a lot about leadership, and you have more possessions. I'm still not sure how you relate to me.

Leader: The good news is that you're beginning to get it. Just one more thing....who are you again?

Follower: Ummm....I'm your follower.

What is a leader? Is it a way of being? Is it related to personality? Is it about whether or not people follow you? Is it different from management? Does leadership have to do with doing the right things, doing things right, or for that matter even doing the wrong things? To be honest, all those ways of defining leadership seem a bit idealistic. If nothing else, they require us to come up with our own definition of leadership and then try to live by it. In some ways, it makes more sense to talk about leaders than leadership. If you are reading this book, you are probably a leader of some kind. In some area of your life you are responsible for other people. They have either put you in that role, or you put yourself there. It might be formal or informal, but ultimately someone is going to look to you to make decisions about where they will go, what they will do, and how things will be organized.

If there is one word I would use to describe leadership it is *responsibility*. If you don't want responsibility, don't lead anything. If you are already a leader, you are responsible for something, and in most cases, for the work, livelihood, perceptions, development, and even the choices of other people. That's why leadership is challenging. Some might say that leadership isn't about being responsible for the behaviors or perceptions of others, but those folks probably haven't led or taken on the responsibility that comes with leading. If you think leading is easy, then chances are that you aren't leading well.

For all these reasons, it makes more sense to talk about leadership as a verb, an action, a state of being. Leadership is to lead. To lead means to know what's at stake and to know that at some level you are accountable for what people think about themselves, what they care about, and where they are going. That's probably why God doesn't spend much time defining leadership in the Bible but tells us stories of leaders and of people in places of formal or informal responsibility for others who are trying to figure it out. As soon as you become a leader, all the formulas change, all the outcomes look a little different. People expect different things from you because you were given or accepted the title leader, manager, executive, pastor, mom, or dad.

It's important to understand this way of thinking about leaders and leadership because if you see how it is different from *not* leading, you are now ready to discover more about what is at stake for leaders and will be able to make better choices about becoming one if you haven't already. The upside of leading is that you get to make choices that impact other people and set the agenda for what's important. The challenge with leading is that you've upped the ante and will now have more to protect. Once you're a leader, it is really tough to go back without sacrificing part of yourself. It becomes easier and easier to wrap your identity in what you lead because every message around you says that leadership is a pretty big measure of success. It's what's important in our world. We pay leaders big money to lead us. We expect a lot. But keep in mind, when you fail, followers will move on very quickly to the next leader. If your identity is closely tied to being called leader, you have a lot to lose. If you understand that your job is not to be called leader, but to lead, there is so much to be gained.

Reflections:
1. Ask four people you lead in some area of your life, at work or in another area, to give you honest feedback about how they would define you as a leader. Tell them your intention is to get their honest opinions so that you can understand how to lead them better.
2. Are you a leader? If so, what does that mean?
3. How would your followers define you as a leader? How would you like them to define you as a leader?

4. What would it take for you to take action, any action, to be the leader you would like to be?

Chapter 2

Three Questions Down

Follower:	Why do you lead?
Leader:	Excuse me?
Follower:	I know a lot about how you lead....or shall I say, how you work. But I'm not sure why you lead.
Leader:	Is this some kind of test? Why I lead isn't important. It's how I lead and what I get done that matters. I lead because I'm a leader.
Follower:	You're obviously doing well at that. But I have one more question.
Leader:	Ask away.
Follower:	Why did you choose to be in a position of accountability for the work and development of other people?
Leader:	Excuse me?

When they had finished eating, Jesus said to Simon Peter, "Simon son of John, do you truly love me more than these?" "Yes, Lord," he said, "you know that I love you." Jesus said, "Feed my lambs."

Again Jesus said, "Simon, son of John, do you truly love me?" He answered, "Yes, Lord, you know that I love you." Jesus said, "Take care of my sheep."

The third time he said to him, "Simon, son of John, do you love me?" Peter was hurt because Jesus asked him the third time, "Do you love me?" He said, "Lord, you know all things; you know that I love you." Jesus said, "Feed my sheep. I tell you the truth, when you were younger you dressed yourself and went where you wanted; but when you are old you will stretch out your hands, and someone else will dress you and lead you where you do not want to go." Jesus said this to indicate the kind of death by which Peter would glorify God. Then he said to him, "Follow me!"

John 21:15-19

R ecently I had a conversation over a cup of coffee with a friend who is in a mid-level executive position in a Fortune 500 company. He is a successful, effective, and valued member of his organization, and he is a Christian. All those around him see a person who is doing well, dealing with the challenges of corporate life as a leader/manager. As our time together progressed, he began to talk to me about the challenges in his leadership. He talked of a team he inherited, a team of people who simply weren't effective and who didn't show much hope for improvement. He expressed dissatisfaction with his organization, a lack of overall purpose in his work, and a weak, if any, belief that what he did was making a difference. Given my need to ask deeper questions, even when inappropriate, I had to ask him a question that haunts me every day: "Why do you lead?" His first response was one I hear often from leaders. It's what I call the business appropriate answer.

The fact is that many leaders in today's world are tired of leadership, leadership talk, and leadership advice. And there is so much of it that it often becomes difficult, if not impossible, to answer the question with any sense of a connection to reality. Therefore, his first answer was safe. He indicated that he had seen the ten-year strategic plan for his organization, and that they were focused on increasing shareholder value while serving their customers and employees.

So I repeated the question. "Why do you lead?" Now, before I explain his response, let me highlight something. In our culture, business or otherwise, it isn't normal to ask a question, receive an honest answer, and then ask the exact same question again without any explanation. However, the question is important. If you are willing to wait in awkward silence long enough, interesting things start to happen.

At the end of the book of John, Jesus has a very important conversation with one of His disciples named Peter. To set the stage for this conversation, keep in mind that Peter was a disciple who had followed Jesus, grown close to Him, learned from Him, and then denied ever having been with Him. He didn't deny an affiliation with Jesus once or even twice. Peter denied being a follower of Jesus three times, and at a time when Jesus was being questioned in ways that would ultimately lead to His death. You can now begin to imagine what may have been going through Peter's mind when Jesus asked him, "Peter, do you love Me?" Peter answered the question honestly and openly: "Yes, Lord, You know I love You." Then Jesus asked him again, "Peter, do you love Me?"

At this point Peter had one of two attitudes to take. The first possibility was that Jesus was either naïve or He didn't hear Peter's response. The other possibility was that when Jesus asked Peter about his love for Him, He was asking whether or not Peter loved Him and whether or not Peter believed that Jesus loved Peter enough to accept him, even though he had denied Jesus on multiple occasions. Jesus was asking, "Peter, do you love Me even though I know you have failed Me?" The second time Peter, probably questioning the question, said the same thing. "You know I love you, Lord." The fact that Jesus asked him again brought Peter a little closer to his own humanity, his doubts, and highlighted the importance of what was being asked. And, by the way, asking a question a second time after someone has already answered it isn't normal in our culture. If you don't believe me, go try it and see how your friends respond.

Leaders face the same challenge when asked why they lead, for a second time. My friend was no exception. His response to the question was one I have heard many times since. He said, "I lead because I was promoted into this position. It was the next logical step in my career to be promoted into a management job, and then to the next. Ultimately, I'm not really sure how to answer that question. What do you mean, why do I lead?" At this point it is likely that my friend felt much like Peter, either dismissing me as failing to listen or not understanding his answer. His ultimate response, however, didn't communicate a clear answer to my question but more of a passive response of leadership being the next logical thing to do. So I asked him the same question again. "Why do you lead?"

Jesus asks Peter a third time, "Do you love Me?" Peter, who is now answering the question at the deepest and most vulnerable level, says, "Yes, Lord, I love You." If you are a leader and Christian, the question of why you lead is critically important and might as well be asked the same way Jesus questions Peter. Jesus follows up these questions to Peter with the statement, "Feed My sheep." In communicating his love, even three questions down, Peter is indicating that he knows what's at stake.

Three questions down, leaders begin to feel what's at stake. Why a leader leads is important. At this level, the question could be restated to say, "Why have you chosen to put yourself in a position of accountability for the work, life, well-being, and development of others?" At this level, leaders begin to see what's at stake. Loving Jesus isn't about Peter; it's a question of whether or not Peter understands what is at stake, what is important, and whether he believes that Jesus demands his real answers. *Do you love Me, Peter, even though I know you have failed Me, and I know you could and probably will fail Me again? Do you love Me even though I know that? Be obedient to My calling on your life.* Three questions down, Peter knows that all he is, and all he is not, is on the line.

Why do you lead?

I lead because I was promoted to this position. I lead to increase shareholder value. I lead because I like to manage others. I like to lead a team.

Why do you lead?

Why are you asking me again? Didn't you like my answer? I lead because I am a pretty good leader of others. I lead because I want to maintain my job security, my retirement, my home, my family's security. I lead because I am trying to live up to something.

Why do you lead?

I lead because I have made a choice to sacrifice myself for others, to develop them, to invest in them, to help them find meaning. I lead because Christ has called me to obedience to Him.

God wants to use you for His purposes in spite of you. When He asks you, "Do you love Me" the third time, He wants the answer that includes all your fears and shame as well as your strengths. When you get to that honest point with Him, He can do amazing things with you. Below are three questions. You will notice that they're ridiculously redundant, but that's the point. Answer them for yourself.

Reflections:
1. Why do you lead?
2. Why do you lead?
3. Why do you lead?

Chapter 3

Whose Are You?

Leader:	I never knew we went to the same church. How cool is that?
Follower:	Yeah, we've been here for the last two years. My family started coming here back when my wife and I were separated. I was in a management position back then, and I was putting my job, career, and all my goals ahead of my family and ahead of God. It was a rough time. I started to feel miserable, even though I was still doing well in my job at work. Eventually I started to hate myself on the inside, and that caused me to turn inside myself. It was a really lonely time for my wife and kids. I got so ashamed that I started to feel like God had forgotten about me. It was a rough time in my life. This community has really changed my life. I don't feel like I have to compartmentalize my work and life anymore, and I owe so much to the loving people in this community who put themselves out there for

me. When I felt miserable, they reminded me
that God loved me anyway.

Leader: Wow, I can relate to that story. It's great to
see you. I need to run now; I have to work
this afternoon. In fact, can you come into the
office today? You know that project is due on
Wednesday.

Follower: Sorry, but I can't. I don't work on weekends
anymore.

Leader: You don't work on weekends?

And a voice from heaven said, "This is my Son, whom I love; with him I am well pleased."

Matthew 3:17

For several years now, I've wanted to try downhill mountain biking. If you've never heard of it or weren't aware that there are different kinds of mountain biking experiences, let me tell you that I now know firsthand that there are. Downhill mountain biking requires you to wear full body armor (shoulder pads, full-faced helmet, elbow and shin pads, and even goggles). And, one of the most exciting downhill mountain biking experiences happens in summertime on the ski slopes in Whistler, British Columbia. On a recent trip to Whistler with three buddies of mine, we decided to rent all the gear necessary to mountain bike on the downhill slopes (including the bike itself) and give it a go. If I failed to mention it, let me also say that this happened to be our fortieth birthday trip with just the guys, so we had something to prove. We also decided to take a three hour lesson with an outstanding guide named Meesh that proved to be the smartest thing a bunch of forty year old guys could do.

While the overall day of biking and the lesson went really well, I'll never forget one particular line that our instructor repeated over and over again as he was trying to guide us and keep us safe on the mountain. Several times throughout the day he said, "Always look where you want to go, because you will go where you look." That statement sounded good on paper, but made even more sense as the day went on. At one point during our ride down the mountain we came across a series of bridges in the woods that were only about two feet wide, but probably five feet off the ground. It was a pretty intense experience going across those bridges as one false turn to the right or left put you into the floor of the woods, and into a combination of stumps, brush, rocks, and tree trunks. As three of us emerged from the woods into a clearing, one of our friends was still navigating the bridges in the woods behind us. A few seconds later as we looked back at the woods from which we had just emerged, we heard an extended yell as if someone was falling about five feet, and then a heavy thump like the sound of a bike hitting a tree and a person hitting the ground. We then called out to our friend to see if he was ok. After a few scary seconds he moaned, "I'm ok, I think."

When he emerged from the woods with a large branch sticking out of his spokes and another smaller branch protruding from his helmet, he said, "Meesh was right. As soon as I looked away from the bridge and looked below the bridge, that's exactly where I went....right off the bridge." As you can imagine, that story will live in our shared memories for decades to follow, and provide a nice laugh for each of us. Meesh's words will not be soon forgotten.

While it's absolutely true that you should look where you want to go because you go where you look, there is also something that must come first. The reality is that we will all fail and fall off the bridge several times during our lives. In order to know where to look, you have to know where you want to go. And, if you know where you want to go, but also that you will fall at many points along the way, what is it that must come before that? You must know whose you are? Knowing to whom you belong may be the only thing that will sustain you when you fail, or even when you are showered with unbelievable success.

The measure of your worth as a leader, your integrity as a person, and your overall effectiveness cannot be summed up in what you achieve? If it were all that mattered, how will we measure our worth when we fall repeatedly? For that matter, could our worth be wrapped up in a proverbial ethic that tells the story of what you did right and wrong, effective and ineffective? Are others drawn to you because of what you do? Think about it. If you could package up all of your results throughout your lifetime, would that be an accurate representation of your contribution to this world? When I consider my own leadership, I certainly hope not.

As you heard this question — "Could your sense of worth as a leader be summed up in what you have achieved and the results you have obtained?" — you may have said, "Of course not!" And then your mind began to dismiss anything I might say next as intuitively obvious and not addressing your needs as a leader. I would urge you to follow up this obvious conclusion with a careful look at how you work, where you spend your energy, what you expect from others, and the assumptions you communicate to those you lead. While you may long for a larger sense of worth as a leader and an opportunity to bring more to your work, many of us still keep our identity in a container full of results, goals met, businesses built, children getting good grades, and kudos from others for all these activities. When people comment on the leaders they admire the most, they often use terms like strong, positive, integrity, honesty, humility, character, and authenticity. While words like ethical, effective, results-oriented, and decisive certainly come up as well, these words are rarely, if ever, enough to put a leader into the "most admired" spaces on our lists of leaders. Why is this so?

Whether you know it or not, your distinctiveness as a leader is less about what you achieve (although valuable) and more about *whose you are*. You might then ask yourself, What does that mean, *whose you are*? When you think about the language we use to describe the leaders in our lives, you realize that leaders "belong" to those they lead. We say things like "my boss," "my dad or mom," and "my pastor." Followers have an ownership interest in those they lead. Thinking about leaders as possessions of their followers changes the way we think about our relationship to those we lead. Just as my house provides shelter and my car provides me with transportation, my leaders provide me with something that helps me either get where I need to go, grow where I need to grow, or something that may protect me when I need it most.

Going even further, whose you are is closely related to who you are or your presence, your way of being, your attitude, ultimately the WHY of your existence. At the beginning of Jesus' ministry, His identity was made very clear to Him and came as a direct message from God the Father. At the time of His baptism, God's statement set Christ's identity in place as His Father's beloved Son. As I have told my students over and over again, I believe their identity cannot be wrapped up in any test score, stock price, grade, or piece of constructive feedback. When I pray for them I pray that God will provide their identity, a greater sense of their meaning to Him, and a greater sense and understanding of His love and acceptance of them.

If you take the time to consider all the roles you play to the people in your life, you quickly realize how connected we are to the experience of others. One way to consider this to peel back those roles like an onion, one layer at a time. Pretend for just a moment that I can no longer be a consultant, a leader, a professor, or any other profession I might enjoy. Now consider that I can no longer be a son, a father, a friend, or a husband. As a close friend of mine once asked, If you take away all those roles in your life, what's left?[1] He and I both agreed that the last question for each of us is the question of whether we believe that God loves us for who we are, both the good and bad parts. In thinking more about that question I realized something else. Most of the time I'm only about 70 percent sure that God loves me completely, but I'm 100 percent sure He loves those around me completely. In an instant, I realized the importance of those around me in reminding me that, at the end of the day, I am a beloved child of God. And now that I understand the most important question, what happens if I put the layers of the onion back?

What I realized is that all the layers look different because of my question and answer at the center. If God loves me completely just as I am, what am I to do next?

In our research with hundreds of leaders in Fortune 100 companies, churches, para-churches, not-for-profits, and different occupations, we found increasing evidence that the most important characteristics of leaders who effectively deal with challenging situations are often more closely related to perspective and attitude than to specific behaviors. Leaders we are willing to follow to the ends of the earth bring something different to their leadership. That something is about how they are with us, their placement of others above themselves, the way they approach adversity, and the way they perceive the future and the past. These are people who have considered whose they are as much as who they are. These leaders have taught us so much about what it means to accept your own identity as a beloved daughter or son of God, an identity that can release you from yourself long enough to see the need in others. I have to remind myself that I often question my own assurance of God's acceptance and love for me. At those times, I am drawn back to my own community of trusted friends and colleagues who can remind me of that assurance. That's why the community that surrounds you is so important. I am 100 percent convicted about God's love for you, but on a daily basis I am probably only 70 percent sure of God's love and acceptance of me. How thankful I am for those around me who remind me daily of whose I am.

As Viktor Frankl, an author who survived the tragic events of Auschwitz, suggests, "even the helpless victim of a hopeless situation, facing a fate he cannot change, may rise above himself, may grow beyond himself, and by so doing change himself. He may turn personal tragedy into triumph."[2] Assuming that the most adverse times create the greatest challenge for leaders, what is it that allows certain leaders to triumph, even in the midst of indescribable adversity? Is it what they do? Or is it the way they perceive their world, their presence under pressure, their ability to be for themselves and for others in the very same moment that sets them apart?

So what are you as a leader to do, or more accurately, to be? And to whom will you belong? The question of who you are is important. Equally important is the question of whose you are. Who do you serve? Who are you accountable to? For what would you be willing to sacrifice yourself, or more precisely, for whom? Because you have opted for the path of leading others, you have a very important job indeed. It doesn't matter what the leaders in your life believe. It's what you believe that matters. The statement "It's not our place to provide meaning in your work" is a ridiculous premise when it comes to leadership. You exist as a leader to build something meaningful for those you lead. You exist to serve and be faithful to the deepest needs of others. Because they spend most of their waking life working for you, you cannot separate their meaning in this world from the everyday ways they are serving others—customers, family members, employees, bosses, and themselves. Granted, they have their own choices to make, but you have a gift as a leader, and an opportunity to develop your people and to help them see potential in themselves and in their work. As a leader, you have the opportunity to offer grace where none is expected and to offer conviction where it sometimes isn't appreciated. Like it or not, the people you lead are watching and listening. You have a daily opportunity to give them something to model, or to model something they will promise never to be. Which leader would you like to be?

Reflections:
1. To whom do you belong?
2. What do you stand for? In other words, what are the two or three principles that define your leadership,

and how do these principles show up in your life and leadership?

3. How would those closest to you describe *who you are*? If you don't know, take the time to ask someone you trust who they would say you are. What would they say you stand for? If they aren't able to tell you anything that surprises you or gives you new insight, ask them again—and ask them to go deeper, or consider asking someone who would give it to you straight.

4. Do you have the assurance that you are a beloved son or daughter of God today? If not, find a trusted friend who can help you come back to that assurance. That friend may need the same assurance from you.

Chapter 4

Dying to Lead

"When you starve with a tiger,
the tiger starves last."

Your attitude should be the same as that of Christ Jesus: Who, being in very nature, God, did not consider equality with God something to be grasped, but made Himself nothing, taking the very nature of a servant, being made in human likeness. And being found in appearance as a man, He humbled himself and became obedient to death—even death on a cross! Therefore, God exalted him to the highest place and gave him the name that is above every name, that at the name of Jesus every knee should bow, in heaven and on earth and under the earth, and every tongue confess that Jesus Christ is Lord, to the glory of the Father.

Philippians 2:5-11

Have you ever stopped in an airport bookstore and taken a long look at the titles on the business shelf? On a recent business trip I did just that. While I hope I don't sound like a complete pessimist, I found the shelf in front of me so unbelievably self-focused that I actually chuckled out loud. The clerk behind the counter asked me what was so funny. We then had a very interesting conversation about the titles on the shelf. In all honesty, I was also attracted to some of the concepts. Who wouldn't be? Some version of the statement "How to find wealth, success, and significance" was staring back at me in the titles of at least 70 percent of the business books on the shelf. Even humility and service were being sold as a sure way to feel significant or even to get rich. Do you see the irony? Headline: *Successful leaders are humble!* While there's nothing inherently wrong with success, wealth, and significance, it's obvious that we aren't that interested in reading something unless it offers us a big payoff.

The fact is that you won't find too many books written about the concept of sacrifice unless it does offer a significant payoff. It's impossible to popularize sacrifice unless there's something in it for us. If it were easy to consider, it wouldn't be much of a sacrifice in the first place. For that reason, it shouldn't be popular. It's tough to sell an idea that suggests outcomes don't come first, survival of your organization isn't priority number one, and that preservation, profitability, meaning, self-actualization, happiness, confidence, and results aren't the point. That's a tough sell. If the concept of sacrificing yourself as a leader was a popular concept, there wouldn't be much at stake. A close examination of Philippians 2:5-11 offers advice that is difficult to swallow but nevertheless offered as a command for leaders who profess Jesus Christ as their Lord and Savior. If Christ is the ultimate role model, who wants to get in line to be crucified? The line forms here, and I assure you, no one will cut in front of you.

First off, your attitude should be like that of Jesus Christ. Okay, I can handle that. Next, Jesus Christ is God, was God, and forever shall be God. But here comes the rub. Even though He was God, He didn't consider that fact something to be grasped or held closely. He let go of the power of His "Godness." Jesus Christ was fully God, yet even He was willing to let go of the power and ego associated with being all powerful. For the Bible scholar or normal business leader, that is tough to grasp. Nevertheless, it is key to our understanding of the attitude God is commanding. Even though Jesus was fully God, He was willing to let go of that fact in order to empty Himself to the point of a servant, for the sake of obedience, and in the face of the most humiliating death imaginable, death on a cross. Jesus was fully God yet chose to let go of that confidence so He could sacrifice Himself for the world. Whatever you need to feel isn't the first priority. God is calling us to humility, to sacrifice ourselves, and to let go. Instead of a nod, that should cause you and me to pause in consideration of the request God is making. The problem is that we often don't even take the time to pause as leaders. We don't have the time.

If you are commanded to take on the attitude of Jesus Christ as a leader, what attitude are you to assume? Think about the things you hold most tightly and be honest about it. Think about the conversations that start your day. Think about those things that cause you to worry. For many of us leaders, the attitude we assume is that of self-preservation, not that of letting go of our all-powerful selves. In essence, if Jesus Christ was willing to let go of His own power and perception of His being the omnipotent Son of God, are we willing to let go of that which makes us, as leaders, the gods of our own lives?

What are you grasping onto as a leader? Do you wake up each morning and consider the things you need to release in order to make obedience to God the center of your life, or do you wake up each day thinking about how to make more money, keep your business in the phone book, get to the next management level, get that promotion, or keep up with your peers? Do you consider the size of your house, your income relative to your peers, the size of your church, the number of people who think you're really a great leader, your level in your organization, the credit you've received, and how to support your lifestyle because that would finally mean you were successful and providing for your family? If you haven't reached the income level or level on the corporate ladder you desire, but you are consumed by those goals, you are in the same boat as others ahead of you.

In contrast, do you wake up each morning offering your life as a sacrifice for the needs of others, in obedience to God? God is asking for that attitude without the promise of riches, comfort, self-actualization, promotion, increased revenue, or an effective team, but with the promise of a heart connected to His heart and the possibility of something eternal occurring in every day you lead. Truly sacrificial leaders would lay it all down for Christ's sake. They are few and far between, but they're out there. They are aware of the temptation to make it all about success as they define and need it, and that awareness gives them an ability to put everything in their lives and leadership on the line for the sake of obedience to God's calling on their lives.

Reflections:
1. Take a moment tomorrow morning before you walk into your workplace to thank God for the opportunity to lead today, and try to make it a habit.
2. What are you most afraid of losing?
3. What if all those fears were gone—what would you do next?
4. Consider two things in your life that are keeping you from being a sacrificial leader, or, if you're a parent, a sacrificial parent. What two things are the most difficult for you to sacrifice, and why are they difficult sacrifices?

Chapter 5

The Relative Unimportance
of Results

Leader:	Just do it.
Follower:	Just do what?
Leader:	Get it done.
Follower:	But what's the point?
Leader:	The point is that I'm responsible for making sure you get there.
Follower:	Get where?
Leader:	To the goals I set for you.
Follower:	For the sake of what?
Leader:	Because we need it done.

> Therefore, God exalted him...
>
> Philippians 2:9

W hat's your daily motivation to get up in the morning, put on your clothes, and head into work? Are you motivated because of what it will get you? At the beginning and end of the day, do you do what you do because it will lead you or others to something great? Are you motivated by goals and outcomes? Is that what comes to mind first when you think of why you work, why you lead, and why you are here?

I must admit that one of my greatest motivators is a big, idealistic dream of what could be. It is often a dream of changing the world in some large and significant way. But if those dreams become my reason for leading and working, I come into a dangerous place because there is also, by default, the potential for my ego to get closely attached to the accomplishment of those dreams. Why not? In the world that surrounds many of us, motivation by outcomes is the focus. You do get to choose your goals, and for some those goals are quite noble. I want an effective team, increased profitability, a healthy organization, a safe and stable financial future for my family, and at the same time I want to feel like I am making a contribution and changing the world. Do you get up and go to work in the morning for the sake of these outcomes, or is it something else?

The apostle Paul uses some interesting words in Philippians chapter 2. After calling us to an attitude that is modeled after the humility, obedience, and self-sacrifice of Jesus, he writes, "Therefore" God exalted Jesus to the highest place. What this passage of Scripture does not say is that Jesus Christ emptied Himself and died on a cross "so that" God would exalt Him. His sacrifice wouldn't have been much of a sacrifice if Jesus had taken the step of self-sacrifice for the sake of being exalted. But those aren't the words Paul uses. Jesus was motivated out of love. His sacrifice was necessary, prophesied, chosen for the sake of love, done out of obedience, and not for the sake of exaltation or the outcomes for Himself.

In our daily work as leaders, outcomes are the culturally acceptable pursuit and oftentimes the very reason for our existence. We are surrounded by goals, targets, metrics, achievements, income statements, sales quotas, performance goals, desired end states, bottom lines, worries, and even failures that constantly remind us that goals and achievements are the point. In our busy world, we often work and work hard *for the sake* of outcomes.

Why is it so difficult to put outcomes aside, even for a moment? Part of the reason is that the achievement of outcomes points toward survival, a fulfilling life, and sustainability. I once asked a group of executives whether or not God cared if their organization survived. It was an interesting question for sure. I was trying to get them to consider whether organizational life is about survival. Do we work *so that* our organizations will survive? Their response was interesting to me because they knew that I teach at a Christian university. They said, "Well, Dr. McKenna, does God care if your university survives?"

To be honest, I still cannot answer that question. But Christ's example calls our very survival into question. Is the point of your organizational life and your leadership survival? Is the point of your life to make sure that your children turn out a certain way, get the best grades, get into the best colleges, and have the most fulfilling life possible? So you serve others *so that* your life will be fulfilling? Do you serve because it feels good? Jesus emptied Himself of His power as God to the point of death for you and me, and therefore God exalted Him. The personal achievement of exaltation wasn't the point. It couldn't be the point. If we are called to this same attitude, what do we do with all those outcomes we pursue every day?

The point is not to beat ourselves up for all the goals we're setting and achieving, but to put them in perspective. Are you doing what you are doing for the sake of you or others getting something, anything, or for the sake of obedience to God's calling on your life? God will surely exalt you for your willingness to put Him first every day of your life, but that exaltation isn't the point.

Reflections:
1. If you consider the possibility that your personal sacrifice as a leader is more important than your success or the success of your organization, how does that make you feel?
2. What are the goals you put first in your life, even the goals for other people or your organization? What if you had to let those goals go today, right now?
3. Look at your schedule for today and all you are supposed to accomplish. If you took the risk to believe that God's agenda was more important than your agenda, how would that impact those things that show up in your schedule? Even if they didn't change, how would it impact what you will do and who you are called to be?

Chapter 6

Is God Showing Up?

Follower:	Excuse me, leader, can I ask you a question?
Leader:	Of course.
Follower:	I know I'm not supposed to talk about things that matter at work, but are you a Christian?
Leader:	Well, as a matter of fact I am.
Follower:	Me too. What difference does that make?
Leader:	Difference in what?
Follower:	For some reason I've been thinking that my belief in a God who sacrificed Himself for me should make a difference in everything I am and everything I do.
Leader:	You might be right, but we have work to do. Let's talk about this when it's a little more convenient.

The eyes of the LORD are in every place, keeping watch on the evil and the good.

Proverbs 15:3

Therefore go and make disciples of all nations, baptizing them in the name of the Father and of the Son and of the Holy Spirit, and teaching them to obey everything I have commanded you. And surely I am with you always, to the very end of the age.

Matthew 28:19-20

And He is before all things, and in Him all things consist.

Colossians 1:17

How does God show up in your life on a daily basis? If you're like me, that's a really tough question to answer, especially on certain days. I'm not a guy who can say with honesty that God speaks to me personally. I have really struggled with that throughout my life. In fact, I can remember a time late one evening when I was in high school lying down in a pasture in the middle of Kentucky and explicitly asking Jesus Christ, the Son of God, to show Himself to me. To be honest, I was scared to death that Jesus—sandals, robe, beard, and all—would show up. I wanted Him to show His face to me and offer me some insight into His plan for my life. To my dismay, He didn't show up. No "face time" with God that night.

Today I still feel the need to see His face in a concrete way. I feel the need to hear His explicit plan for the world and for my life. But most of the time I don't feel or experience God's presence that way. At times I feel like Jesus is a friend who drops a letter in my mailbox once in a while but doesn't sit right next to me and have a conversation with me. Other times I feel even more distant. At one point I had a friend who was contemplating suicide and describing how mad he was at God. I admit with some embarrassment that instead of listening to his story I was thinking, *Man, I am so jealous that he's close enough to God to be mad at Him.* Keep in mind that my friend was contemplating suicide. (We'll talk about my selfishness later...I'm sure your mind never wanders when someone else is talking☺)

Today my perspective looks a little different. Although God hasn't come to me in my waking hours and spoken to me, I see and feel His presence at very interesting times. I see God's presence when I read the Bible to my kids at night, when I interact with those who have needs, when I sing, when I teach, and when I choose to pay attention. That last part is important. I feel God's presence when I turn my head just far enough to not only read Scripture, pray, and worship, but when I begin to believe that God might actually be present in even the most mundane and ungodly parts of my day.

I read an interesting quote a couple of years ago that still sticks with me today as a leader. Karl Holl describes calling in our lives as "awareness of God's presence in every moment of life."[3] To use Solomon's voice in Proverbs, "The eyes of the LORD are in every place, keeping watch on the evil and the good." What's interesting about this passage is how often we assume that God shows up in the evil, shameful parts of our lives to judge us, but how rarely He might show up in the good. Regardless, for me that was a stretch. I believed it in theory, but what if I believed it in the practice of my daily leading? I began to think to myself, *What if I believed that were true? What if I believed that Jesus Christ was present in each and every moment of my day?* That would mean that every moment, every conversation, every business challenge, every failure, every time I screw up, when I teach graduate students, the time I spend reading and responding to email, the time I spend making business decisions, and the time I spend making my to-do list had the possibility for something greater to occur or even something eternal. It's always been easier to see God's impact and presence in my wife and children, but could He actually show up in the typical aspects of my day as well?

So I thought I'd try it out. Three or four days a week (Why not seven? Because I'm not that good!) the first thing I do is get out my schedule for the day and pray this prayer: "God, if You are going to show up when I am reading my email (or insert your own task or meeting), I am open to that, and I pray that Your will comes before mine." Then I spend a little time thinking about the different things I am doing and what might be important in the lives of those who may somehow be impacted. If I'm not sure how God is going to show up, I just ask for His will, not mine.

Here's what's interesting. When I began to do that, several things happened. I must admit I did see small miracles here and there. I began to see possibilities that I didn't see before. Call it a self-fulfilling prophecy or call it God's will, I think it's both. I began to get more focused on what was eternally important, and I am sometimes able to get outside myself long enough to see those in need, and especially those I can have an immediate impact upon. On a selfish note, I think I have become a little more interesting as a person because I had a chance to reflect on what's important and meaningful in each interaction of my workday.

But it does require some discipline and the risk of God showing up in your entire life (work, leadership, family, and all) and reflecting on that possibility. He's showing up and has an agenda for you to review. Are you willing to pay attention? To be honest, I'm often not willing and that's the choice that God gives me. It's my choice to make that time, even when I am too busy, stressed out, or leading too many people—especially when I am too busy, stressed out, or leading too many people. God is here. Does that make a difference to me?

Reflections:
1. What if you believed that God was going to show up in every moment of your work today? What would that mean? What would you do differently?
2. Do you want to see God's face? Are you willing to take the time to let Him show you a few things? If so, when will you take that time? Make the commitment to a specific time right now, even if you will feel guilty when you miss it once in a while.
3. Where is there space in your life for intentional time with God? You don't have to over spiritualize it, just consider where in your day you can spend time in open and honest reflection and prayer with God. If you've never done it, commit to fifteen or twenty minutes a day and see what happens.

Chapter 7

Don't Let the Gift Go to Your Head

"I wouldn't say that my bullying boss was unpopular as a child, but her parents had to tie a lamb chop to her leg just so the dog would play with her."

"So now, go. I am sending you to Pharaoh to bring my people the Israelites out of Egypt." But Moses said to God, "Who am I, that I should go to Pharaoh and bring the Israelites out of Egypt?" And God said, "I will be with you. And this will be the sign to you that it is I who have sent you: When you have brought the people out of Egypt, you will worship God on this mountain."

Exodus 3:10-12

Moses said to the LORD, "O Lord, I have never been eloquent, neither in the past nor since you have spoken to your servant. I am slow of speech and tongue." The LORD said to him, "Who gave man his mouth? Who makes him deaf or mute? Who gives him sight or makes him blind? Is it not I, the LORD ? Now go; I will help you speak and will teach you what to say." But Moses said, "O Lord, please send someone else to do it."

Exodus 4:10-13

When we think of having a gift, we often think of that gift as a strength, a competency, or a personal attribute that makes us really good at something. To the contrary, a gift is something we have been given that provides the opportunity to think, be, or do something with that gift. Otherwise it wouldn't be called a gift. If God has given you the gift of leadership, it means that He has provided you with the opportunity to lead. You have the opportunity to shape the experience of others, to invest the resources to provide something of value to your customers, employees, family, church, community, and other stakeholders in your life. You get to make decisions about how it will go for those you lead. You get to call some of the shots that others may only complain about. What an incredible opportunity. For that reason, it's always impressive when I run into people who have chosen *not* to take the opportunities offered them to be in positions of leadership. While some of them may not have received that opportunity, others simply don't want the gift.

The Bible is full of references to leaders who were given the gift of leadership but expressed very little competence, confidence, or experience necessary to lead well. Just a short list leads you to the stories of Abraham, David, and Joseph. Jesus Himself was at times reluctant to receive the leadership opportunity provided Him, yet each of these leaders changed the world, are remembered for their incredible accomplishments, and the courage they portrayed in leading others. Moses is another obvious addition to the list of reluctant leaders in the Bible who received the gift from God. When God calls Moses to lead, Moses immediately brings up his inability to speak eloquently and questions why anyone would listen to him in the first place. God's message to Moses is clear and humorous. God says, "Who gave man a mouth?" Is there any chance that the Creator of mouths could work with the ineloquent mouth of Moses? God seems pretty sure He can provide for Moses. Having the gift of leadership means being responsible for someone else. You're not an accountant keeping track of the details of others' lives, or a historian writing the story of the people in your life. You have real, down-to-earth, love-it-or-hate-it responsibility for the work and development of someone else.

Once you were offered and accepted your gift of leadership, what were you then called to do? You now have the realities of being a formal leader or manager. You manage budgets, evaluate the performance of others, hire and fire, manage projects, make decisions regarding disciplinary action, and you get to set the agenda for how and what work will be done. In the role of manager you also get the blame when things go wrong, but that's a small price to pay for the possibility of making a difference that may last for eternity. Deep down you probably are aware that you don't have what it takes to lead anyone or anything, but the Creator of mouths has the power to keep you moving forward toward His agenda.

While it may be difficult to connect God's agenda and your faith to your daily business activities, it doesn't have to be. If it is that difficult or you feel a value conflict in your work that won't let you go, maybe you should change jobs. For most of us, however, it means making a commitment to put God in control and seek to live our beliefs out in real time in our work. For some of us, that means investing the time in prayer and contemplation of our true values. If your business and personal success come first in your life, then your value system may not be something to contemplate. But if you believe that God has gifted you to lead for His purpose, then you have an exciting opportunity to create spaces for a message of hope, love, and grace to those you lead. While you are responsible for chasing the goals in your life and work, you have the opportunity to make choices about the worldview that will drive your decisions and the decisions of those you lead.

Reflections:
1. If you consider the idea that while you may have the "gift of leadership," that gift is an opportunity that was given to you whether you deserved it or not, how does that impact your perspective on your leadership?
2. If you have received the gift of leadership, what fears emerge when you consider the possibility that God could use you to further His kingdom through your work?
3. If you mentioned these fears to God in prayer, what humorous response would He provide to you? God

said to Moses, "Who gave man a mouth?" What would He say to you?

4. If you believe that God provided you with the opportunity to lead, what are three things He might be calling you to be or do today?

Chapter 8

Successful Leaders Have Much to Carry

Leader: I just bought a sailboat, and I'm wondering if you can come help me get it launched this weekend. I can't get it off the trailer, rigged, and in the water by myself. I also bought a new truck to pull the boat and a GPS system to get me to the boat launch. The whole thing is a little stressful because my wife wasn't completely excited that I bought the boat. She's afraid it's just one more thing that will keep me away from being fully present at home. They say the worst day in your life as a sailor is the day you buy the boat, and the best day is the day you sell it. I wish I had understood that before I bought the stupid thing.

Follower: I'm sorry to hear all that. Is there anything I can do?

Leader: I'm so glad you asked.

A champion named Goliath, who was from Gath, came out of the Philistine camp. He was over nine feet tall. He had a bronze helmet on his head and wore a coat of scale armor of bronze weighing five thousand shekels; on his legs he wore bronze greaves, and a bronze javelin was slung on his back. His spear shaft was like a weaver's rod, and its iron point weighed six hundred shekels. His shield bearer went ahead of him.

1 Samuel 17:4-7

Do you remember the first time you received a paycheck that provided more income than you could dream of ways to spend it? For me, that paycheck came in the first year of my marriage. Not only was the paycheck more than my bills and planned spending combined, it also came at a time when my wife was drawing a nice salary as well. We had no children and were making a combined salary that far outreached our immediate spending needs. It was an awesome feeling. What's funny is that if we had stayed at that level of income, it would be very difficult if not impossible for us to pay our current monthly bills now ten years later. Inflation aside, as our income expectations have adjusted to new levels, our personal expectations for our lifestyle have also been difficult to keep in check. The more we have succeeded, the more we have had to carry, and ultimately the more we have to lose.

Leadership isn't all that different. Do you remember the first time you were put in the position of managing someone else? If you are a parent, do you remember the feeling you had when you first saw your child? Do you remember all the excitement of being a new parent, combined with all the fears because you realized you knew nothing about being a parent? Whether a first-time manager or a new parent, now you had the incredible opportunity to be responsible for the work and development of someone else. As a manager, you could now be the kind of manager you wish you had been managed by in the past. As a parent, you could now put all of your working theories of what it takes to be a good parent directly into practice. As a manager, you would now be able to talk about the people you hired and fired, how other people were responsible to you, and about all the courageous things you had done in dealing with the realities of managing people. Whether you are a parent or a manager, the more success you have at leading these significant others in your life, the more you will accumulate and carry, and the more you have to protect.

Even parents have a lot to carry. As our kids get older, we measure our success by their grades, their position in the band, their position on the cheerleading squad, how fast they are, and how smart they are. The pressure to have kids involved in everything is unbelievable. If your kids aren't involved in overlapping sports, taking karate, excelling at school, and batting .500 in T-ball, you're a failure as a parent. The more they succeed, the more we as parents have to protect.

In business terms, leadership success is often measured either by the net revenue or profit of your business, or by the number of people you lead. People are impressed by the numbers you maintain and by the victories that got you there. What they may not see is all you have to carry to feed the imposter inside of you that knows you are just a normal person trying to lead in a very complex and challenging world.

Those who have seen you succeed expect you to continue succeeding, have a nicer office, more money, less time for the little guys in your organization, and more power. They expect you to speak with conviction and without fear, and to push on without thought of defeat. You become invested in your success. Your identity as a parent and as a leader can easily become tied up in the perceived success of the role. As a successful leader of others, it will take a small army just to keep you successful.

The story of David and Goliath has revisited me several times in recent years because I am the father of two boys. Goliath is a beast of a man, an evil adversary to our hero David. He is the giant to be slain that will lead us down a path to greatness. Small boys relate to this story. In David, they can see the possibility of slaying the giants around them and becoming heroes, even though they are just boys in a world of men. While David is the obvious role model because he defeated the giant and stands for the hero in all of us, if you have seen success and value it deeply, it's Goliath that may represent more in you. Successful leaders don't often look or act like shepherd boys. Successful leaders look and act like giants among us. They wield incredible power and surround themselves with all the resources to protect their leadership, as well as the people to make their leadership possible. They also have big voices that challenge all competitors to compete with them, and tell followers to respect and fear them. Strength and conviction take the place of humility, authentic fear and doubt, and childlike ignorance of just how vulnerable we are.

The story of David and Goliath is an unlikely lesson for each of us. If you are a successful leader, there is little doubt that the Goliath in you is there. Even if you aren't a Goliath leader, be aware of how you cheer on the Goliaths around you and miss out on the Davids all around. You don't get invited to serve on influential boards for most organizations or even churches unless you have been a successful leader, a big name, or a big pocketbook. You won't get pursued by headhunters for senior leadership roles unless you have made a great deal of money for your organization. You won't be invited to be a keynote speaker unless you have made it in some way. In rare cases where we can see the measurable difference in outcomes, sacrificial leaders are lifted up, but they are rare cases. Organizations breed success and protect it once they have it. It's human to do so. That said, success is not inherently bad. In fact, we need people with the courage of Goliath. A track record of goal achievement isn't a bad thing. The problem is that a track record of success often gives you so much to carry and protect that there is little time for reflection on why you are leading in the first place.

It is interesting to imagine how the story would have finished if Goliath had taken off his armor, dropped his spear, told his assistant to go and grab a bite of food, and bowed before David. It would have required an unimaginable awakening in the heart of Goliath and the courage to ignore his success, size, and power long enough to see the real story of God's power unfolding before him. Can you imagine yourself surrendering all that you have accomplished for the sake of God's unfolding plan?

Being a manager or executive isn't about a great title, more money, or more influence. Being a manager, executive, or parent, for that matter, means more responsibility, an understanding that there is more at stake for others, and a willingness to lead for the sake of God's calling to serve Him and love others in serving Him. The pressure in your daily life is often to work toward the protection of all that you have and for the possibility of having more. Having creates a balancing act in each of us because it isn't inherently evil or bad, but it creates more and more to carry, and therefore more and more to protect. Do you live for the sake of protecting what you have and having more, or for the sake of God's good and perfect will for your life? That's a good place to start.

Reflections:
    1. If the description of Goliath, his armor, and the support needed to keep him going were replaced

with a description of you, how would the description read?

2. As you consider what it would take for you to bow before God right now, what are the actual possessions you would have to lay down? What are the dreams or aspirations you would have to surrender? Who around you is making you feel like your success should be protected, lifted up, and celebrated? What would it take for you to be known as a leader who was always willing to surrender success and affirmation for the sake of serving God's plan for your life?

Part II

The Question of Identity: Whose Are You?

Chapter 9

Reluctance to Lead

Leader 1:   Thanks for coming today. As you know, we've been looking to fill this position for the last six months. We were excited to meet you. You have all the right experience and your educational background is very impressive. Can you tell me a little about why you're interested in this position?

Leader 2:   To be honest, this job fits me and will help me get to the next level. I want this job because I am resourceful and productive, and this job fits with my career goals. I want this job, and I'm looking forward to being hired.

Leader 1:   You seem pretty confident. Are you sure you're thinking about this job? You'll be responsible for the future, work, and development of one hundred people.

Leader 2:   Oops, sorry. I thought I was interviewing for the leadership position you posted.

Then Jesus went with his disciples to a place called Gethsemane, and he said to them, "Sit here while I go over there and pray." He took Peter and the two sons of Zebedee along with him, and he began to be sorrowful and troubled. Then he said to them, "My soul is overwhelmed with sorrow to the point of death. Stay here and keep watch with me."Going a little farther, he fell with his face to the ground and prayed, "My Father, if it is possible, may this cup be taken from me. Yet not as I will, but as you will."

Matthew 26: 36-39

On a recent business trip to Pasadena, California, a long walk through the city brought me to the campus of Fuller Theological Seminary. In the center of their campus is a bronze, life-size statue of Jesus being nailed to the cross. While I have often imagined the scene, this sculpture showed me something different. Instead of lying on the cross and waiting for the nails to be driven into His hands and feet, Jesus' back is arched away from the cross and two individuals are leveraging all their strength and bodyweight to hold Jesus down. Jesus' face communicates despair, fear, and obedience all in the same moment, and the arching of His back along with the anticipation of the coming pain shown in the flinching of His hands and feet brought me to my knees in tears. In that moment, I was again faced with the reality of my Savior, who experienced every bit of pain, fear, sadness, insecurity, and hurt that comes with sacrifice and obedience, and with being human. Jesus was fully committed to the will of God the Father, and He was fully willing to communicate His reluctance to bear the burden of dying on the cross.

What do you want from a leader? Even a brief look at the lists of leadership competencies organizations seek in their current or next leaders highlights the importance of conviction, skill, savvy, vision, connection to others, courage, ethics, and in some cases, humility. There is one more trait that should be added that doesn't show up on many of these lists: a reluctance to lead. How in the world could anyone suggest that a key leadership competency is a reluctance to lead? First off, a reluctance to lead is not a fear of leading but a true awareness of what's at stake for those you lead. It's also an appreciation for the responsibility associated with leading others. Anyone who has served as a leader knows that the position comes with a great cost and great challenge. If you don't believe it, ask any leader who has been through a significant leadership challenge that impacted their overall identity, their confidence, their character, and in some cases their reputation in a significant way. Leaders who have been to the depths understand what's at stake for them and for those they lead.

If your leadership is about you and your survival, you probably don't understand the concept of reluctance as a strength. The reality is that leaders who make their leadership about them or those close to them and miss the opportunity to serve others don't understand the cost because they have focused their attention on reducing the costs. Leading well is hard work, and a realistic leader will express a true reluctance to lead along with a message that says, "I know it will be tough, but I am supposed to lead."

Let's be honest, it takes an incredible amount of courage and self-awareness to communicate reluctance. Just think of your last job interview. If you felt it, did you communicate any reluctance to the person interviewing you? In your defense, reluctance is often seen as a lack of conviction or a lack of courage. However, in the spirit of honesty, shouldn't we be willing to express reluctance if we're feeling it, without fearing that those talking with us will see us as wishy-washy, fearful, or a misfit for the job?

Jesus understood reluctance better than anyone. During the time He was in the garden, He expressed His own reluctance to face both the personal burden and pain of His pending death, and the incredible weight of His sacrifice for the sins of the world. While Christ understood the necessity of His sacrifice for the world, it still was not something to be grasped as part of His ego. He was to bear the weight of this truly unbelievable burden alone, truly alone. This is the second reason that a reluctance to lead is important and necessary. The sacrificial leader may get no glory on earth, may actually be blamed in situations where he or she does the right thing but can't share all the details of the situation, may step back behind the curtain so that others might be glorified, and ultimately may take on many challenges alone, very alone. Get in touch with that and you will understand the importance of a reluctance to lead. Leading can be a lonely business.

For leaders, reluctance is healthy, necessary, courageous, and connected to the stakes in the job. Nevertheless, leaders will still take the risk for the sake of providing an opportunity for others, for the sake of obedience to and love for God, and for the sake of something greater than themselves. A reluctance to lead should be on every organization's list of core competencies because it's at the core of every leader's character. Sadly, you won't find it on any of the lists. You may find humility, but you will rarely, if ever, find reluctance to lead.

Look for a reluctance to lead in yourself and in those you hire. Look for people who want to lead but are reluctant because they know what's at stake. One way to uncover this in yourself is to identify what you would do if you couldn't lead anything. If you had no more responsibility for others, no more vision to cast, no more way to influence others, and no more power to wield, how would you feel? This will help you understand how tightly you hold on to leading as part of your identity. Watch for a false sense of humility in yourself and others. Humility doesn't require a name. Those who are reluctant just are. You can be reluctant and confident at the same time. True leadership means wanting it like nothing else and being willing to leave leading behind if you aren't needed anymore. That's a tough line to walk, but a necessary line. The fact is that many are reluctant to lead but aren't willing to be honest about it, because organizations aren't looking for reluctance. For most leaders, budgets aren't fun. Managing others oftentimes isn't the most exciting part of leading. That's because some of the people you lead will be incompetent, unable to get the job done, reactive, blamers, entitled, or tired. You will also get to manage great folks, but that won't be all of them. But you still must lead. You are responsible for the work and development of others. You know what's at stake.

Reflections:
1. Why is there a lot at stake for leaders? Why is there a lot at stake for you as a leader? If you are considering leading or managing others, what makes you reluctant to take on that role?
2. What was your greatest leadership failure, and why do you consider it a failure? What did you learn from the situation that may have made you stronger and better to serve as a leader today?
3. If you couldn't be a manager, executive, parent, pastor, or leader at all, what else would you do?

Chapter 10

The Courage to Be Irrelevant

Follower:	For Christ's sake!
Leader:	What did you just say?
Follower:	I said, for Christ's sake!
Leader:	Did you just swear at me?
Follower:	I don't think so. I just realized why I'm here. I'm here for Christ's sake. I've been acting like I'm here for my sake. I had it all wrong. I'm here for the sake of my God, Jesus Christ, who sacrificed everything for me.
Leader:	You sound like a new person.
Follower:	I am, and I'm living for Christ's sake.

"I am deeply convinced that the Christian leader of the future is called to be completely irrelevant and to stand in this world with nothing to offer but his or her own vulnerable self."[4]

Henry Nouwen
In the Name of Jesus

Can you imagine this job posting: "High-tech company hiring for a mid level executive with the experience and skills to take the business to the next level. Five to ten years of management experience in technology and systems integration. Global leadership experience preferred. And one more thing: Must want the job and be reluctant to take this responsibility, and must have the courage to be irrelevant, even if it costs her or him."

I recently had the opportunity to present at a first-level management training seminar in a Fortune 100 company. The audience was a group of young, new managers, all aspiring to executive-level leadership and looking for any tips on how to negotiate their corporation's leadership ladder. The speaker before me was a mid-level executive who had been through a significant derailment experience that had set him back for several years. Ultimately, he had failed to say the right thing at an opportune moment when presenting to a group of top executives in the company. This setback caused him to be blacklisted for promotion into more senior leadership roles because, as he explained, he had opened his mouth at a critical moment in a meeting in front of the top brass in the business.

He went on to describe his difficulty getting back on track after sinking for several years, eventually emerging into a role where he has stayed without the possibility for further promotion. He had come to the end of his career in the business but had learned lessons the company wanted him to pass on to these new managers. His advice to these young leaders was simple. "Know the political landscape of the organization so you will know what is and what is not appropriate to say." That was the jewel he left with these young leaders. What a jewel.

If you have chosen to lead others, there is no doubt that the people who surround you, follow you, and have power over you have helped to establish a culture that communicates what is and is not acceptable, and what will be tolerated. That's the reality. Political understanding and behavior is a necessity in a leader's life, but the pressure to be relevant, acceptable, appropriate, to dress the right way, say the right things, ask the right amount of questions, and toe the right lines for personal and organizational gain at all costs can be a dangerous thing for the leader dying to lead. Not dangerous because of ethical dilemmas (although a reality), but dangerous because these cultures are based on the achievement of outcomes and often do not reward the sacrificial behavior that Henry Nouwen described as the courage to be irrelevant.

The courage to be irrelevant is the courage to look at your own problems before seeing the mistakes of others. It is the awareness that you are called to make a difference in the lives of others. It is the courage to see corporate politics and to put them in perspective, never forsaking love for power. It is like a mother who looks to teach her children about taking a risk for God to see those in need around them when her friends and family encourage her to protect them, provide everything for them, and set them up to take care of themselves first. She, like the leaders with the courage to be irrelevant, can see God's sometimes uncomfortable calling to an irrelevant, grace-filled, and other-focused life.

Henry Nouwen, in his book *In the Name of Jesus*, describes this as the courage to be nothing but our vulnerable selves. Why did he connect irrelevance to vulnerability? At the core of our character is an honest notion of who we are and who we're not. Assuming each one of us has made and will continue to make mistakes, and is realistically fearful about the future, irrelevance takes courage. Talk with any business leader and you'll quickly see the powerful role that being perceived as relevant plays in our daily life. Each and every one of my business clients demands that anything they do be completely relevant to the "business case" or relevant to the goal of making money. The problem is that in many cases, the honest truth is that we aren't competent enough to do the job, we are fully aware of our limitations, and we aren't able or willing to communicate all these feelings. To communicate them honestly would mean being seen as irrelevant, off the point, and as a weakness. While I hesitate to connect the courage to be irrelevant with success, I will say this. In some cases a willingness to be vulnerable and honest does pay off. Humility and vulnerability are so rare in business that an honest dose from someone is seen as so refreshing, it's actually rewarded sometimes. However, Nouwen isn't suggesting that leaders be irrelevant and vulnerable for the sake of success, but for the sake of being real and truthful about all that they are.

Reflections:
1. If you defined the courage to be irrelevant for yourself, how would you describe it?
2. Think about the competing tensions of being relevant and appropriate while also being irrelevant, courageous, and inappropriate. In what ways does the pressure to be relevant hinder you?
3. What is one thing you could do today that could be seen as irrelevant in human terms but completely relevant on God's terms?

Chapter 11

Steadfast

"I'm not fickle or wishy-washy, I'm just exciting."
—Unknown (and should remain that way)

Surely he will never be shaken;
a righteous man will be remembered forever.

He will have no fear of bad news;
his heart is steadfast, trusting in the LORD.

His heart is secure, he will have no fear;
in the end he will look in triumph on his foes.

Psalm 112:6-8

When I think about the most important mentors in my life, I often think about a man named Kim Gara. To his students, he was Professor Gara. To me, he was one of the most important influences on my life and career as a professor and businessman. While Kim and I didn't always agree, I respected him for the strength of his convictions and even more for the motive behind his convictions. He was about service. He understood sacrifice as a leader, and if I had to pick one word to describe his presence with me, it would be *steadfast*.

Kim was nearly impossible to shake. He was serious about his work with students and businesspeople, yet he also laughed at his own silliness with a calm and contagious chuckle that I can still hear today. His steadfast presence often showed itself in his eyes. When he looked at you, he was attempting to understand and lead you, but his eyes always communicated an unshakeable faith in you and in his God. The tragedy of Kim's influence in my life is that he died of a stroke at the age of fifty, yet he left a marker and inspiration in my life that I carry forward. At Kim's memorial service, hundreds of people commented on his humor, guidance, friendship, love of others, and mentoring. I will always remember him for that steadfast look in his eyes.

The Psalms are full of prayers for a steadfast heart–a heart that is unshakeable, faithful, obedient, humble; a heart like a rock in the face of trouble. A prayer for a steadfast heart is not a prayer for success. Leaders who are steadfast are the foundation that holds an organization and its teams together. They provide structural integrity to the emotional and reactive rollercoaster of organizational life. When attacked, the steadfast leader may respond firmly and with the precision of a surgeon, but without the reactivity of a juvenile. A steadfast heart is not a heart without doubts, concerns, questions, or failures, but a heart that has been offered as a sacrifice for others and a heart that is intentional about putting trust in God at the top of the agenda.

Recently, upon catching my own eyes in the mirror, I was reminded of Kim's eyes. While I usually would have looked away from the familiar stranger in the mirror, because looking at yourself is embarrassing in a weird sort of way, I couldn't help but wonder whether those I lead see a steadfast person in me and a person whose hope, fear, and trust is in his God. I'm not sure, but my aspiration for a steadfast and faithful presence lives on. That is Kim's leadership legacy to me. He wasn't a strong and unshakeable presence in my life because he was confident in himself, but because he had surrendered his life to his God, he understood sacrifice, he accepted God's grace, and he did it for the sake of others.

Reflections:

1. Take a moment to look at yourself in the mirror. More specifically, take a moment to look into your own eyes. What do you see? Do your eyes reflect a leader who is present, connected, and steadfast, or a leader who is moving on to the next thing, reactive, and trying to get it all done on your own terms? If you see the former, keep looking at yourself long enough to experience the awkward fact that you are

looking at yourself, and pray for God's strength to give you a steadfast heart.

2. If you were unshakeable and had no fear of bad news because of your hope in God, how would you be different today? If you were a steadfast leader, what is one thing you would do differently today that would impact those you lead?

Chapter 12

Who Are You, Really?

"A person who smiles in the face of adversity...
probably has a scapegoat."

"If you can stay calm, while all around
you is chaos...then you probably haven't completely
understood the seriousness of the situation."

The LORD sent Nathan to David. When he came to him, he said, "There were two men in a certain town, one rich and the other poor. The rich man had a very large number of sheep and cattle, but the poor man had nothing except one little ewe lamb he had bought. He raised it, and it grew up with him and his children. It shared his food, drank from his cup and even slept in his arms. It was like a daughter to him.

"Now a traveler came to the rich man, but the rich man refrained from taking one of his own sheep or cattle to prepare a meal for the traveler who had come to him. Instead, he took the ewe lamb that belonged to the poor man and prepared it for the one who had come to him."

David burned with anger against the man and said to Nathan, "As surely as the LORD lives, the man who did this deserves to die! He must pay for that lamb four times over, because he did such a thing and had no pity."

Then Nathan said to David, "You are the man! This is what the LORD, the God of Israel, says: 'I anointed you king over Israel, and I delivered you from the hand of Saul. I gave your master's house to you, and your master's wives into your arms. I gave you the house of Israel and Judah. And if all this had been too little, I would have given you even more. Why did you despise the word of the LORD by doing what is evil in his eyes? You struck down Uriah the Hittite with the sword and took his wife to be your own. You killed him with the sword of the Ammonites. Now, therefore, the sword will never depart from your house, because you despised me and took the wife of Uriah the Hittite to be your own.'"

2 Samuel 12

Self-awareness is often defined as the realization that you exist and awareness of your strengths and limitations, your relationship to others, and your place in the world. It is often cited as a critical ingredient when we define leadership competence. We want leaders who understand themselves well enough to look for strength in others when theirs is lacking, and for strength in themselves it's needed. But what are we looking for when we say we want leaders who are self-aware? Do we want them to be aware of their passions and convictions? Do we want them to know their label according to the latest leadership profile? Or do we want something more?

In many cases, self-awareness is simply defined as knowing yourself. The question is in how self-awareness is generated in a world where we are constantly encouraged to listen to our own voice, to be convicted at all costs, to be intolerant of evil in others, and to demand ethical and moral behavior and thoughts from our followers. The conversation between King David and the prophet Nathan is an interesting one. As far as we can tell, David is a good king with some very real human flaws. At one point in his life, David makes a big mistake and then covers it up. He sleeps with the wife of one of his soldiers, she gets pregnant, and then he makes multiple attempts to cover his tracks that end in the murder of the woman's husband. Even in the face of a very obvious parable that parallels David's mistake almost to the point of being ridiculous, David still isn't aware that Nathan is describing him. You have to read this with a slight chuckle as you realize how ridiculous David sounds. Nathan's parable is direct, implicating, and barely a degree away from

David's actual behavior, and he doesn't even see it coming. He has no idea that Nathan, without much effort at all, is luring him into a trap that David ultimately sets and triggers himself. *The man deserves to die!* In all his conviction, you can almost imagine David saying "I deserve to die!" without even missing a beat, and in so doing, convicting himself to death.

It's a silly story for leaders, right? David is someone to be mocked for his foolishness, his sin, and his stupidity. Or is he? Are we far from that type of foolishness? The challenge with self-awareness is that it constantly eludes us. When we think we have found it, we become most dangerous to those around us. We become the very thing we spot so easily in other leaders we follow — unaware, driven, sure of the problems in others, focused on data and not ourselves, and really dangerous as leaders. While David's repentance comes quickly and humbly, the consequences of his mistake are set into place. God forgives David, but the consequences for him and his household are severe.

For that reason, self-awareness is something to be sought, but to be sought with the caution necessary to never quite arrive. To arrive at self-awareness would be like the greyhound finally catching the artificial rabbit at the racetrack. If the greyhound catches the fake hare, it goes crazy and must be destroyed. What if we believed we had finally caught up with our own self-awareness? What would that look like? If you arrive at that point, on a self-awareness scale from one to five, you will be a five. If you find yourself there, take a quick step back and start again.

My favorite definition involves so much more than an awareness of yourself. It is an awareness of how other people see you. When I ask leaders whether or not they are self-aware, what I am really asking is whether they are aware of how other people see them and how they see themselves. All the awareness in the world means nothing if everyone else would say, "He says he's a good listener? Ha, he couldn't hear his own voice unless it was right in front of his mouth!" Self-awareness requires you to stop and ask others, even others you don't particularly like or appreciate, how they see you. You also need some trusted voices. But to really understand how you are perceived is to complete the picture of who you are.

It's a tough question to ask. If you have ever been disappointed after listening to yourself on tape or watching yourself on video, you will know what I mean. Becoming aware of our complete self and how others perceive us is usually painful and healing in the same moment. It's tough because what we hear isn't what we wish we sounded like, and it's healing because we get closer to a realistic perception of who we really are. David was no more a fool than you or me. Because of that, we can learn from him. I have a feeling he would suggest we get real about knowing ourselves and look to the Nathans in our world to give it to us straight.

Reflections:
1. Do you know how other people see you? Pick five people 1) one trusted peer 2) one enemy 3) one person who reports to you 4) one mentor, and 5) one close friend or your spouse. Ask them to give you three of your strengths and three of your weaknesses. Tell them you are trying to be more honest with yourself and others, and let them teach you about you.
2. Next time you hear a speech, listen to a sermon, or read a good book, discipline yourself to only think about yourself and what the speaker or author might be telling you. Completely avoid the temptation to relate the words to someone else you know. If you have difficulty doing this exercise, you really need to keep trying.

Chapter 13

The Right Stuff

Follower 1:	I've been thinking about taking a management job lately, but I'm a little worried that I won't like it. I've heard from others that until you get into a formal position of leading others, you really won't be able to get it. They also told me that stepping into a job where I lead others will change my perspective. I'm not sure how, but I think I want to try it out. What do you think?
Follower 2:	I've heard the same thing. Someone told me it's like parenting. Like the moment your kids came into this world and all the questions in front of you changed. As a father of two kids, I get that. When my kids were born, it was weird. It was weird because I didn't really know them yet, but I was immediately willing to throw myself in front of a car for this little person who entered my life in a moment. All the questions and answers changed for me in that moment. Suddenly I was responsible for

protecting this little person, and at the same time, I was responsible for letting them experience life on their own and take their own risks.

Follower 1: That's a great story, but what does it have to do with whether or not I should become a manager?

Follower 2: On second thought, maybe you should consider jobs that don't involve other people.

The elders who direct the affairs of the church well are worthy of double honor, especially those whose work is preaching and teaching. For the Scripture says, "Do not muzzle the ox while it is treading out the grain," and "The worker deserves his wages." Do not entertain an accusation against an elder unless it is brought by two or three witnesses. Those who sin are to be rebuked publicly, so that the others may take warning.

I charge you, in the sight of God and Christ Jesus and the elect angels, to keep these instructions without partiality, and to do nothing out of favoritism.

Do not be hasty in the laying on of hands, and do not share in the sins of others. Keep yourself pure.

Stop drinking only water, and use a little wine because of your stomach and your frequent illnesses.

The sins of some men are obvious, reaching the place of judgment ahead of them; the sins of others trail behind them. In the same way, good deeds are obvious, and even those that are not cannot be hidden.

1 Timothy 5:17-25

Leading is a dangerous job. A recent article in *Fast Company* magazine[5] highlighted the most dangerous executive job in the corporate world as that of the chief marketing officer (CMO). The article indicated that while it is less likely that the chief executive officer (CEO) or the chief operating officer (COO) will be let go, the CMO is always one bad marketing campaign away from losing his or her job. Sometimes it's no fault of their own, but simply a mismatch between leader and company or being in the wrong industry at the wrong time.

When corporations discuss their high-potential leaders, the first thing they often emphasize is the appropriate range, scope, and breadth of experience. Does the leader have the experience necessary to lead our organization at the next level, in this particular business, and at this time in our industry? The danger of overemphasizing a leader's resume is that we miss some of the most likely leadership pitfalls that will not only cause problems for the organization, but might cause setbacks that last for years to come. The point is not to deny the importance of experience but to highlight it as the wrong place to start. So where should the leadership search begin? One possibility is to redefine the core organizational leadership competencies that drive us.

Most businesses now have a list of their core competencies. In the last three or four decades the identification, communication, and evaluation of leadership and organizational competencies have changed the way we think about leadership and our businesses. Lists of competencies, abilities, and skills are the backdrop for leadership excellence and organizational sustainability. The attainment and exhibition of these competencies are used to interview, select, develop, evaluate, and even fire leaders. They are used to highlight each organization's business niche and non-negotiables, and their identification is often the trademark of new CEOs and senior leaders. Identifying the core competency of an organization is known as the way to identify the things it must be doing to be effective, successful, and still in the phone book a few years or months from now.

Competencies vary from level to level and from job to job. First-level managers must do different things than the executives leading three or four levels above them. Executives leading an organization of several thousand employees have to let go of the competencies that made them successful as first-level managers leading a team of seven or eight. There is no doubt that leadership competence in managing others, building teams, developing others, translating and communicating vision, and formulating strategy are absolutely critical, and this is just a start.

Take a quick look at the indicators of success or failure in today's leadership climate. A glimpse at the most popular business and leadership publications tells us something about what we as a culture want in leaders. In most cases, we're looking for leaders who will help us become what we desire, leaders who will take our organization to the next level, cause us to innovate, to grow, to find our vision, and who offer us something better than what we are now facing. Churches and other not-for-profits aren't excused from this pursuit either as they often look for leaders who will sustain them, grow them, or help them identify and fulfill their mission.

One challenge is that lists of leadership competencies are as fickle as the leaders who create them. You're always one CEO change from an entirely new set of organizational values and leadership competencies. In one day, all that you've done that was seen as so good can be immediately seen as bad and off the mark. In an organizational climate like that, is there anything about leadership we can hang our future on? What would such a list of time-tested leadership competencies look like, and where would we find them? Would this universal list be competencies, skills, attributes, or abilities? Or would this list be about character? Maybe character is what we're really looking for in leaders, especially if defining the necessary competencies is such a moving target.

John Stott, commenting on 1 Timothy 5, identifies five qualities needed by Christian leaders in their dealing with others for whom they are responsible:

1. Appreciation—affirming outstanding performance
2. Fairness—not listening to unsubstantiated accusations
3. Impartiality—avoiding all favoritism
4. Caution—not reaching hasty decisions
5. Discernment—looking beyond the outward appearance to the heart

Stott writes, "Whenever these principles are in operation, mistakes will be avoided, the church will be preserved in peace and love, and God's name will be protected from dishonour."[6]

Consider how popular business publications would appear if these qualities were the top priorities. The qualities in this list, if exhibited by a leader, don't guarantee we will become something spectacular, but they guarantee gratitude, fairness, impartiality, patience, and discernment. We love to hate these characteristics in our leaders because leaders like this are just so darn levelheaded and difficult to shake. Let's be honest, it's difficult to imagine such a leadership approach being popularized, but why? Simply put, leaders like this are real, connected to the needs of others, and tough to shake, but they may not make us richer, more self-actualized, or more mission-focused. Yes, they may ask us to be better people and exhibit these competencies ourselves, and ultimately we may crucify them for it.

Leaders of the kind of character Paul suggests are often sabotaged because their character is rarely our reason for hiring them in the first place. Even when we ask for leaders of character, we want it only if we can defend it as a means to our organization's survival and prosperity, and toward our own personal gain. If you think that portraying these qualities in your own leadership is easy, I challenge you that it simply is not. To be connected to the needs of others and still hold onto yourself is difficult work. That's why sacrificial leadership is tough work. If you think you lead this way and the ability just comes to you, it is likely that you aren't really working at leading well, but rather practicing what you know and what makes you comfortable.

Reflections:
1. Rate yourself on the five competencies below.

Competency	Definition	Rating (1 low, 5 high)
Appreciation	Affirming outstanding performance	1 2 3 4 5
Fairness	Not listening to unsubstantiated accusations	1 2 3 4 5
Impartiality	Avoiding all favoritism	1 2 3 4 5
Caution	Not reaching hasty decisions	1 2 3 4 5
Discernment	Looking beyond the outward appearance to the heart.	1 2 3 4 5

2. Have a person who knows you and gives you honest feedback rate you on the five competencies below.

Competency	Definition	Rating (1 low, 5 high)
Appreciation	Affirming outstanding performance	1 2 3 4 5
Fairness	Not listening to unsubstantiated accusations	1 2 3 4 5
Impartiality	Avoiding all favoritism	1 2 3 4 5
Caution	Not reaching hasty decisions	1 2 3 4 5
Discernment	Looking beyond the outward appearance to the heart.	1 2 3 4 5

3. Discuss your personal rating with the ratings of your trusted other. Where were the ratings the same? Where

did they differ? What are your obvious strengths? How would you lead differently if you improved your scores in one or two areas?

Chapter 14

Leaders Are Dorks

The new executive stood before the paper shredder looking confused.

"Need some help?" a secretary asked.

"Yes," he replied. "How does this thing work?"

"Simple," she said, taking the fat report from his hand and feeding it into the shredder.

"Thanks, but where do the copies come out?"

"But what about you?" he asked. "Who do you say I am?"

Simon Peter answered, "You are the Christ, the Son of the living God."

Jesus replied, "Blessed are you, Simon son of Jonah, for this was not revealed to you by man, but by my Father in heaven. And I tell you that you are Peter, and on this rock I will build my church, and the gates of Hades will not overcome it."

Matthew 16:15-18

For anyone not familiar with the term *dork*, it is a term my wife and I often use to highlight the quirkiness, eccentricity, pickiness, laughableness, nerdiness, and utterly ridiculous qualities we see in each other and in ourselves. The other thing about dorks or dorky people is that they often are fully aware they are dorks. Dorks are nerds, comics, accidents waiting to happen, and often only funny to themselves. Most importantly, they are able to laugh at their own dorkiness, their limitations, and at the imperfect manner in which they conduct their lives.

My wife and I use the term for each other because it highlights something that brought us together in the first place. After ten years of marriage, we both tell the same old ridiculous jokes, repeat certain sayings, and laugh at ourselves in ways that most often can only be greeted by one response: "You are such a dork." While some might find the comment hurtful, we are both aware that part of our love for each other is grounded in our willingness to laugh at ourselves, and even at each other, because we both know that once we begin to take ourselves too seriously, we lose our ability to keep things in perspective. We would lose our ability to see our own limitations and to keep ourselves from getting entrenched, enraged, and unwilling to budge for the sake of the person to whom we are married.

Let's get one thing clear right now. Leaders are dorks too. Leaders do ridiculous things every day. They make mistakes that cost organizations a lot of money. They take ridiculous positions that are indefensible because they are afraid of looking stupid. And when they are really feeling the pressure to succeed, they take themselves way too seriously. Consider this for a moment. Every successful and unsuccessful leader you know was once an elementary school kid on the playground. Each one of them was trying to establish his or her identity from an early age in life and carried with him or her the challenge of being taken seriously while avoiding the temptation to take themselves too seriously. Many of those school kids are now the leaders of organizations, impacting the lives of people under their responsibility. While they have more experience now and are often caught in the seriousness of the adult world, inside they are all still dorks just like you and me.

The biggest danger we face as leaders is taking ourselves too seriously, losing sight of the playground child that still lives in each one of us. Leaders who take themselves too seriously build too much confidence in their own ability to get the job done, and they often develop a tunnel vision and hardheadedness that doesn't allow them to rebound back to reality when things get tough.

Parents aren't excused from realizing their inner dorkiness. My wife gets in a good laugh about half the time I discipline our kids in the car. I usually use words that my kids don't understand yet (they're only five and six) like respect, discipline, no monkey business, and "if you don't stop hitting your brother, there'll be consequences." To which my younger son says, "There'll be counting sentences?"

The upside of admitting you're a dork is the fact that in the Bible God chose dorks most of the time over their more qualified peers. Over and over again God chose people who realized that their continued obedience and connection to His purpose was closely tied to their awareness of their meager and often ignorant origins. Peter was no exception. If anything, Peter took himself a bit too seriously. When Jesus asks His disciples who they say He is, Simon Peter quickly proclaims Jesus the Christ, the Son of the living God.

Because of the importance of the Bible as God's Word revealed to us, we often lose sight of the ironies revealed in the lives of biblical characters. While many assume that Jesus' renaming of Simon to Peter, meaning *rock*, establishes Peter as the foundation for the leadership of the early church, the irony is in the fact that Peter also was such a blockhead at times. Unfortunately, he often took himself so seriously that his overconfidence got him into trouble later. Jesus was aware of the irony in Peter's title and eventual leadership, but Peter had to learn his lessons the hard way.

Let's face it, we are all dorks when it comes right down to it. The inner schoolchild in all of us is still there. The only difference now is that when we realize our limitations we make one of two choices. We either embrace the child by laughing at how silly we are in all our selfish ambitions, or we hide behind a false sense of confidence that brings out the reactive, hurt, and self-preserving child we should have left on the playground years ago.

Reflections:
1. When you were an elementary schoolchild, what was your greatest fear when you were on the playground? If your greatest fear was that the other kids would see how dumb you really were, how unpopular you were, or how difficult things were for you, consider how those fears might still be impacting you today. If you accepted the fact that everyone is just trying

to compensate for their own "inner dork," could you begin to laugh at yourself more freely?

2. Do you take yourself too seriously? When you feel frustrated, are you able to just let other people take over for a while?

3. Think of the most ridiculous thing you've said or done in the last two days and go tell a friend about it and have a good laugh. Most likely they will share a similar story with you.

4. Have the courage to be a dork with those you lead. God doesn't take you that seriously, so why should you?

Part III

The Question of Perspective: How Do You See It?

Chapter 15

You Do Have a Choice

Three mates die in a car crash, and then they go to heaven and attend an orientation meeting.

They are all asked, "When you are in your casket and friends and family are mourning for you, what would you like to hear them say about you?"

The first bloke says, "I would like to hear them say that I was a great doctor of my time, and a great family man."

The second says, "I would like to hear that I was a wonderful husband and schoolteacher who made a huge difference in our children of tomorrow."

The last fella replies, "I would like to hear them say... Look, he's moving!"

In the process of writing this book I have had dozens of conversations with business acquaintances, clients, pastors, and friends about the concept of dying to lead. One of the most difficult questions I've had to deal with is "For the sake of what?" For the sake of what do you lead? For the sake of what have you chosen to be responsible for the work and development of others? For the sake of what do you live? If Jesus' example is our guide, then the answer is simple, and incredibly complex. Jesus Christ as our example offered Himself as a sacrifice for the sake of an undeserving world and to glorify God.

As I have already suggested, outcomes cannot come first in this way of thinking. Our leading isn't for the sake of our business success or survival, for the sake of ourselves, or for the sake of our security. However, this troubles many leaders, Christian or not, for one simple reason. Many leaders believe they often don't have a choice to put outcomes in any place but first. I must lead for the sake of our business outcomes because those above me have set the agenda. What about those times when I don't have a choice?

Without going into all the intricate details, research, and examples of what choice is about, I have one simple question. What is it that makes you feel you don't have a choice? To be fair, I'll tell you what comes to my mind. I don't have a choice to put God's agenda ahead of my business agenda because others have power in my life, and the power to make things difficult for me. My spouse has that power. My boss has that power. My kids have that power. At times, those I lead have that power. And at other times, I have that power over myself. They can make things difficult for me if I choose to surrender myself every day to God's agenda and then figure out what outcomes are important after that. I don't have even five minutes to ask God to step into the details of my schedule today, because ultimately the power that others hold over me is more powerful than the power I would like God to have in my life.

So you don't have a choice? Sorry, you absolutely do have a choice. Let's be honest, when it comes right down to it, we have choices that we simply aren't willing to make "for the sake" of our business, our security, our credit, our paycheck, our followers, our reputation, or our will. There is more credibility in admitting that than in the statement that you and I don't have a choice. Even Viktor Frankl in his book *Man's Search for Meaning* found choice in situations that many of us will never begin to imagine. While in the Nazi concentration camps and when every choice imaginable had been taken away from him, he said, "I could always choose my attitude." The Nazis could take everything away from him, but they could not take away his ability to choose his attitude. You have a choice.

Reflections:
1. What are three choices you think you don't have today as a leader? Now consider what you could choose in each of those situations.
2. What if you decided you were willing to put God's agenda first in your life, even without knowing what that is today? What choice would you have the courage to make that could have a significant impact on those you lead?
3. Look at the highest priority in your work this week and give it to God. Whether it is a major client meeting, a layoff, an interview, or a presentation, take a few minutes and give it to God in prayer. If it is difficult to pray that way, just repeat this. "I give [your priority] to You, Lord. I give [your priority] to You, Lord. I give [your priority] to You, Lord." A little repetition never hurts.

Chapter 16

What's That to You?

When you have three young boys it is hard to know who to blame when something goes wrong in the house. One father explains how he solves the problem:

"I just send all three to bed without letting them watch television. In the morning, I just go after the one with the black eye."

Peter turned and saw that the disciple whom Jesus loved was following them. (This was the one who had leaned back against Jesus at the supper and had said, "Lord, who is going to betray you?") When Peter saw him, he asked, "Lord, what about him?"

Jesus answered, "If I want him to remain alive until I return, what is that to you? You must follow me." Because of this, the rumor spread among the brothers that this disciple would not die. But Jesus did not say that he would not die; he only said, "If I want him to remain alive until I return, what is that to you?"

This is the disciple who testifies to these things and who wrote them down. We know that his testimony is true.

Jesus did many other things as well. If every one of them were written down, I suppose that even the whole world would not have room for the books that would be written.

John 21: 20-25

The funny thing about human beings is that as much as we are motivated for selfish reasons and looking for control over our own lives, we spend much of our time focusing on areas where we have little or no control. We complain about our organizations because they don't provide what we think they should provide. We complain about pending layoffs after we have been told they are coming instead of focusing our attention on how we can prepare for our next job in a new business. We gossip about our peers, team members, or bosses who are causing trouble for us without much thought to what we should do to improve our situations with them. We talk about our friends and the poor job they are doing raising their children without much thought about how we might help them. When we consider providing developmental opportunities for those we lead (or for the children we are raising), we spend unbelievable amounts of energy on blaming the organization instead of what *we* can do right now to improve the situations of those in our care. Why is this so?

Interestingly enough, the conversation between Jesus and His disciple Peter at the end of the Gospel of John gets right to the heart of this matter. Jesus has just asked Peter three times, "Do you love Me?" The conversation up this point probably produced a lot of pressure for Peter as his response was questioned twice and then finally received by Jesus. After Jesus takes Peter deep in His questioning, Peter bounces right back to the surface with a question to Jesus. Peter asks Jesus what is going to happen to another disciple. Jesus' response is direct and comes without hesitation. "What is that to you?" Jesus redirects Peter's meaningless and ultimately selfish question away from the other disciple and back on Peter. What is that to you? Peter's question is meaningless because he wants to focus on someone else and on something over which he has absolutely no control.

It doesn't matter who you are, how much power you have, the size of your budget, the revenue you generated last year, or whether you are parent or friend of the year. When you get under pressure, you, just like me, and just like Peter, are more likely to focus on the three or four things you can't control versus the one hundred things you could change in an instant. I once spent a day with a handful of very powerful leaders with more budget control and power than I can begin to describe. They were talking about the challenge of creating an engaging organization for their employees, where every employee might have the opportunity to engage in meaningful work, to develop personally, and to make a contribution to something bigger than themselves. Throughout the day, I noticed that while this group of leaders could change thousands of things with the snap of their fingers, they spent 99 percent of their energy on the very few things they could not control. In their defense, they were under tremendous pressure. But they could change the experience of their employees in the blink of an eye. Even the most powerful like to talk about their lack of control when they are under pressure. I've often thought how they would have responded if I had used Jesus' words and said, "What is that to you?"

Blame and gossip, while seemingly about other people, are simply ways for us to make everything about *us* without having to do anything to improve us. For many of us, the thing that needs to die in order to put God's agenda first is the focus on things we can't control. To focus on things within our control, every time we want to talk about a situation that involves someone else we should instead end the conversation with a simple statement or response directed to ourselves. *What am I going to do about it? What conversation am I going to have? What am I going to do to put myself aside and be obedient to God's call to love others and Him?* This doesn't mean you become a doormat, because responding to God's agenda for your life doesn't mean you don't matter. But we must die to ourselves daily to let God's agenda prevail each and every day of our lives. The irony of control is that when we get under pressure, when our leadership matters most, our need for control will increase but will most likely increase toward things we couldn't control anyway.

Challenge:

I dare you to spend the rest of your day without talking about one thing you can't control UNLESS you follow it up with, "What am I going to do about it?"

Reflections:
1. Consider how much time you spend talking, complaining, or gossiping about your organization, your boss, your peers, your friends, your family, or your subordinates. This includes any time you talk about anyone without the follow-up thought or conversation regarding what you are going to do about it. Now ask yourself, "What are those things to me?" Get on with the things you can control.
2. Think about the one thing in your life that is causing you the most pressure right now. Write down all the things or people in the situation that you wish would change in some way. After you have the list, cross off all those items over which you have no control, trying to narrow down the list to three to five things you could change tomorrow that would make the situation better.

Chapter 17

Embrace Your Inner Nobody

"It is not sufficient to be a success; it is also necessary for your friends to be failures."

One day Saul said to David, "Here is Merab, my eldest daughter. I want to give her to you as your wife. Be brave and bold for my sake. Fight GOD's battles!" But all the time Saul was thinking, "The Philistines will kill him for me. I won't have to lift a hand against him."

David, embarrassed, answered, "Do you really mean that? I'm from a family of nobodies! I can't be son-in-law to the king."

1 Samuel 18:17-18

Now when the LORD spoke to Moses in Egypt, he said to him, "I am the LORD. Tell Pharaoh king of Egypt everything I tell you."

But Moses said to the LORD, "Since I speak with faltering lips, why would Pharaoh listen to me?"

Exodus 6:28-30

When we think of great leaders, we often think of people who are smart, informed, aware of their place as the leader, emotionally and intellectually connected, and street smart. We think of leaders who have made the right, ethical, and informed choices. If they have failed, they were smart enough to learn from their failures so that they were able to succeed when they faced those same challenges in the future. We often think of leaders who are humble, but rarely do we put naiveté on our list of great leader characteristics. Humility is one thing, but a youthful ignorance is certainly not a characteristic we look for in our leaders. What if we did? Under what circumstances would a naïve, ignorant soul be our choice as leader?

When God chose David to lead His people, He chose someone who by many accounts was ignorant and naïve.

Sometimes when I read about the life of David, I'm dumb-founded by what I see as his laughable stupidity. I'm not just saying that to make a point about God's ability to use even the most ignorant people. Young, and even old, David often sounds like a fool when you see his responses to those around him. The examples are endless. It shouldn't be a surprise when you consider that this young shepherd boy was willing to go up against the greatest warrior in the Philistine empire. While he certainly had faith, he also showed an ignorance and disconnect with reality that was somehow used by God. It makes no sense to imagine that little David could defeat this mighty warrior, but he believed he could, and God used him.

After Saul tried twice to kill David with a spear, he once again plotted to kill David. In this particular plot, Saul wanted David to marry his daughter Merab. Saul's idea was to have David bring him a gift of one hundred Philistine foreskins as a dowry for his daughter's hand in marriage (that's right, Saul wanted foreskins as a dowry. Bear with me, these were different times). First, Saul had already tried to kill David. Second, it was an obvious setup. And finally, David's response is ridiculous. When I read his response, I want to read it in my best backwoods, dippity dog accent. "King Saul, you don't mean that, do ya? I cain't do that, I ain't nobody." The hardest part of all is that as far as I can tell, David really means it. He doesn't feel worthy of the king's daughter. His naiveté is sweet, yet troubling.

Why in the world would God pick a leader like this? It's not the only example in Scripture. The leaders God chose are rarely those we would choose. Imagine David's interview with a Fortune 500 company.

"David, tell me why you should lead our company?"

"Well, ma'am, I'm good with a slingshot, I play the harp, I'm from a family of nobodies, and I don't stand up for myself, especially if someone else is in a powerful position."

"Really, can you give me an example of a time you didn't stand up for yourself?"

"Certainly, ma'am. There was the time my manager tried to get me fired and everyone saw it coming. He actually tried to take me down several times, and I didn't really do anything."

"Why didn't you stand up for yourself?"

"Well, ma'am, he was my manager."

"What about your mentors? What do they think of you?"

"That's a good question. The guy who discovered me—his name was Samuel—he thought I was a runt from the start. He was probably right."

"Thanks, David, we'll get back to you about the job."

David had at least one important strength. He always embraced the fact that deep down inside he was a nobody in his own eyes. When God blessed him, he didn't feel entitled to that blessing. He knew he didn't come from the best leadership stock, with the best experience base from which to draw, or from parents who had served as military leaders or in government. He was aware that he was really nobody, except that God had called him, anointed him, and planned his legacy.

There is little around us that encourages us to consider that God's blessings are His to provide. God certainly rewards obedience and blesses those who are obedient to Him, yet they rarely consider that blessing something to grasp, to be earned, or to seek. In David's case, the blessing was given and David didn't fully grasp God's reasoning for providing it. Maybe he was naïve. Or maybe he had his priorities in order.

Reflections:

1. When was the last time you said "I don't know" to those you lead or to someone who leads you without

following it up with an answer, explanation, or justification? If you say it has been a while, or you have never said it, why not? There is no doubt that you "don't know" in many situations. What would be the impact of an honest "I don't know" the next time you don't know the answer? How would your manager respond? How would your team respond? Consider the possibility that they might actually find it refreshing.

2. If you have been blessed in any way (financially, relationally, physically, materially), do you feel like you deserve it? If so, why do you feel entitled to God's blessing? David served God throughout most of his life and still felt like a nobody, an imposter, someone who received God's blessing simply because God chose to bless him. He was aware of that. Are you?

Chapter 18

Thank God He's Not Fair

A guy phones up his boss but gets the boss's wife
instead. "I'm afraid he died last week,"
she explains.

The next day the man calls again and asks for the
boss. "I told you," the wife replies,
"he died last week."

The next day he calls again and once more asks to
speak to his boss. By this time the wife
is getting upset and shouts, "I'VE ALREADY
TOLD YOU TWICE, MY HUSBAND,
YOUR BOSS, DIED LAST WEEK! WHY DO
YOU KEEP CALLING?"

"Because," he replies laughing,
"I just love hearing it."

My people are determined to turn from me.
Even if they call to the Most High,
he will by no means exalt them.

How can I give you up, Ephraim?
How can I hand you over, Israel?
How can I treat you like Admah?
How can I make you like Zeboiim?
My heart is changed within me;
all my compassion is aroused.

I will not carry out my fierce anger,
nor will I turn and devastate Ephraim.
For I am God, and not man—
the Holy One among you.
I will not come in wrath.

Hosea 11:7-9

When was the last time you knowingly acted in a way that was unethical, immoral, selfish, or sinful not only by your own standards, but probably by the standards of others? If you aren't aware of the last time, you may think more highly of yourself than you should for your own good or for the good of those around you. Now consider the last time that someone you lead did something you consider unethical, selfish, immoral, or sinful. What was your response to their action? Were you appalled at such action? Did you take the necessary steps to discipline them for their wrong-doing? Was the discipline you provided fair in response to the wrong they had done? Was there any part of you that thought to yourself, *You know what, I've actually made the same mistake myself, yet I'm having to discipline this person because they got caught and I didn't?* In these situations, fairness would have convicted you as well as them.

The fact is that life's not fair, and we can all thank God that He's not fair. If God were fair, our daily selfish actions would condemn us to the wrath and punishment we deserve. Like children, our tendency to make everything about us, our financial gain, our popularity with peers, and our own pleasure, would put us in time-out so much of the day that we would scarcely have time to lead anyway. The problem is that God isn't fair. When we suffer or our loved ones suffer, we call out to God because we believe we or they deserve better. The problem with pain and suffering is that while it is difficult for us to comprehend it as a "God allowed" component of life, it is also the suffering, the potential for suffering, and the dark side of life that make God's grace so apparent and necessary. The other inherent complexity in life is our natural tendency as human beings to demand fairness (or justice), especially for others. Demanding fairness for the honest accounting of our own lives is another story.

The book of Hosea has often been described as a beautiful account of God's unconditional love for people. In it, God describes the repeated and knowing transgressions of His children and His anger at the way they have turned their backs on Him and toward their own self-serving agenda. While His anger toward their actions is made clear in Hosea, He refuses to unleash the wrath they deserve and instead acts like God, with compassion that is aroused at the simple thought of His children. God feels it all. He understands what it means to create human beings with the potential to turn their backs on Him, to have them do just that, to consider their "fair" destruction, and to show compassion instead. He understands that man's ways are different from His own, yet He puts up with the silly and clearly deviant actions of His people as they fail Him over and over again throughout the Old Testament. His statement is clear. His people deserve wrath, yet because He is God, they receive compassion once again.

The challenge with the book of Hosea is not to look at the failings of Israel and relate to God's compassion and love for them, but to read the book, look in the mirror, and consider God's compassion and love for you today. You have to consider a love that is given in full understanding that you and I will fail Him again, and more than likely, fail Him today. We won't fail Him in an abstract or general way, but fail Him today by turning to our selfish needs and wants and away from His calling on our lives to serve Him and those He loves. In all the ways we see flaws in others, from the person who cut you off on the way to work, to the person you manage who is letting you down, consider God's way with you. You and I cut God off every day and we let Him down all the time, yet He says, "I'm God and not man; I can't help but be God. You don't desire fairness for yourself. You want fairness and justice for others, but if you are honest, you want preferential treatment for yourself. You are human." Thank God He's not.

Reflections:
1. If God treated you fairly, what would He do to you? Why do you deserve that outcome?
2. If you are someone who is overcome by shame instead of a need for God to do nice things for you because of how good you are, how would you feel if you believed that the grace and compassion God expresses in Hosea was meant for you?
3. If you had the courage to offer grace instead of fairness to someone in your life who has let you down, what would you do next?
4. How can you impact those you lead today by communicating God's compassion in place of your human need for fairness?

Chapter 19

Who Made This Day Possible?

A preacher was lying in bed one night, looking up at the moon and the heavens, and he thought to himself, *Where the heck is my ceiling?*

There are many things about parents that make children squirm. In fact, I bet I can still make you squirm today. Why does the thought of your parents having sex make you nauseous, put you in immediate denial of the birds and the bees, and cause you to scream out, "Please stop!" On a lighter note, imagine the inappropriate words, songs, jokes, one-liners, or clichés that come out of your parents' mouths at just the wrong times. Parents can be racially inappropriate while trying to keep up with the politically correct language of the modern world, or bottle all of pop culture into one phrase, "Oh, kids these days."

My parents are no exception. Or should I say, my reaction to the antics of my parents is no exception. One of my most vivid memories from my childhood is that of my parents singing at the top of their lungs, "This is the day (echo…and yes they would sing the echo) that the Lord has made (echo), we will rejoice (echo), and be glad in it." You may know the song, echoes and all. In my house as a kid, this song was sung most mornings—if not the entire song, some portion of it. The song was embarrassing when friends came over, annoying to my teenage ears, and such a blessing as a permanent imprint on my now adult brain. My parents' message was clear. God made this day possible. We will be thankful for it and joyful in it, even when we don't feel so thankful or joyful.

Being grateful for every day is a nice concept to imagine, but near impossible to practice when it is needed most. Gratefulness comes easily to leaders when the blessings are obvious, when you feel rejuvenated, and when everyone else around you is either grateful or having too much fun to care. Leaders seeking thankfulness are seeking it every day, when their organizations are struggling or succeeding, when their teams are performing or disappointing, when their kids are thriving or failing, and when their answers are clear or their questions are many. If you are human, times when gratefulness to God is impossible will come, but how will you be defined? Will you be bitter or grateful for your opportunity to lead?

Think of a failing, derailing, mistreated, underpaid, or undervalued leader you know. In the same moment, imagine that leader is a grateful leader who still sees their blessings. What would that person say?

This situation is unbearable. I deserve better. My company doesn't know what they have or had. But, at the end of it all, God gave me this day to breathe, to learn, to love, to serve, to enjoy, and to lead another day. This is the day that the Lord has made. I will rejoice, I will lead again, and I will be glad in it. And I will ask myself: in all its pain, possibility, joy, lessons, and challenges, who made this day possible?

My hope today is that I am making my two little boys squirm just as much as my mom and dad made me squirm. If I could only be such a blessing to them, what a blessing that would be.

Reflections:
1. On a scale from 1 to 10, 1 being bitter and entitled, 10 being grateful and glad, how would you rate yourself? How would others rate you? How can you increase your score by two points in the next six months?
2. Make a list of five people you are grateful for. Pick the first five that come to your mind and send them a note, email, or phone message telling them why you are grateful for them.

Chapter 20

Fear, Grace, and the Unlikely Leader

Great truths about the complexity of life:

1. Raising teenagers is like nailing Jell-O to a tree.
2. There is always a lot to be thankful for if you take the time to look. For example: I'm sitting here thinking how nice it is that wrinkles don't hurt.
3. One reason to smile is that every seven minutes of every day someone in an aerobics class pulls a hamstring.
4. Middle age is when you choose your cereal for the fiber, not the toy.
5. If you can remain calm, you just don't have all the facts.

Then King David went in and sat before the LORD, and he said:

"Who am I, O LORD God, and what is my family, that you have brought me this far? And as if this were not enough in your sight, O God, you have spoken about the future of the house of your servant. You have looked on me as though I were the most exalted of men, O Lord God."

1 Chronicles 17:16-17

If you want to understand the complexity of the human condition, try to lead someone. If you want to understand the need for grace, try to lead someone well. The famous hymn "Amazing Grace" written by John Newton in 1748 gets me every time I hear it. I sing through the first verse, which so many of us are familiar with, and then I am led into the second verse—a verse that challenges all of me and presents the beautifully complex and overly simplified idea of grace.

> *'Twas grace that taught my heart to fear,*
>
> *And grace my fears reliev'd;*
>
> *How precious did that grace appear,*
>
> *The hour I first believ'd!*

I've often wondered what exactly Newton had in mind when he wrote this verse. It presents grace as doing two competing things at once. Grace teaches my heart to fear and grace relieves my fears and sets me free. How can that be? How can grace do those two things at once? God's grace is wonderful, simple, miraculous, and incredibly elusive. It's not elusive because God has hidden it from us, but elusive because we hide it from ourselves. Our shame, self-pity, pride, and selfishness make a freely given grace something that is nearly impossible to comprehend. We want to simplify God's grace by making it human and reducing its complexity to a simple formula: Right action acted out = God's grace freely given. Grace comes freely from God, but we are often afraid to receive it because it brings fear and relief, love and evaluation, acceptance and risk. Could grace provide fear and relief? Could your ability to offer grace provide freedom, love, fear, and respect to those you lead?

Newton perceived that God's grace taught his heart to fear. We are comfortable with the concept that the fear of punishment, fire and brimstone, and negative outcomes teaches our heart to fear, but how could the concept of grace teach us to fear? God's grace is given without the necessity for anything from us. In our limited human minds where results and goal achievement are so center to our organizational and personal success, grace without an investment or action is incredibly complex.

It's even more complex when you consider that grace also sets us free. From God's perspective as the one extending grace to us, it is very simple. Newton was most likely suggesting that we are well aware that we deserve *no* grace, that we have failed God and others, and we know we will probably fail them over and over again, but God's grace is offered to us in spite of that. In our world of professional and college coaches who have a job if they win, CEOs who turn over as often as we change cubicles, and where finishing first is often the only acceptable place, a freely offered grace is challenging. Leaders who are aware of the daily challenge of releasing control to God for their work and family probably understand it as well as anyone. There is nothing you can do to deserve God's grace. You have screwed up and you will screw up again. Grace like that highlights our imperfections at the same moment that our acceptance of it sets us free.

John Newton based his famous song on 1 Chronicles 17:16-17. David understood God's grace. In this passage of Scripture, God communicated to David all that He was going to do for him through his ancestors. David, even at this later point in his leadership over the nation of Israel, still understood that God's grace did not come because of his family, what he had accomplished, or what God thought he would still do, but simply because it was given. David was faithful and obedient most of the time, but as a leader he also possessed a healthy understanding of God's blessing and grace, and in the same moment a respect and fear of the all-powerful God of the universe. David's comment, "Who am I, O Lord God, and what is my family, that you have brought me this far?" shows David's unending awe, fear, and appreciation for the grace of God. He goes on to say, "You have looked on me as though I were the most exalted of men, O Lord God." David's statement here highlights his awareness that God is offering him grace as though he deserves it, and he knows he doesn't. God's grace flows freely to us, and we don't deserve it. That's scary.

The complexity of this is critical for us to understand as leaders. Living the life of a sacrificial, obedient, and loving leader requires something more. It requires the acceptance and willingness to struggle with the complexity and ultimate simplicity of God's perspective. What would your leadership look like if you modeled a grace that deserved respect and offered freedom to those you are responsible for? Your grace as a leader gives your followers the opportunity to choose right or wrong, to make mistakes or to succeed, to deceive or to come clean, to support you or sabotage you, and to let you down or make you proud. That possibility makes the grace you extend something risky for you, but that's just the point. God's grace sets you free, allows you to grow, creates possibility, offers acceptance, and sets you free to love others. At the very same moment, that kind of grace highlights your need for grace like a black light on a public bathroom sink. Grace, like that black light, highlights the impurities that sit on our backs as leaders. That same grace cleanses us and offers us a new start every day of our lives. That kind of grace doesn't make sense in our business world today. It calls us to accountability and sets us free each time we confess our humanness to God.

If you are dying to lead, you must be willing to consider the very simple presence of God's grace in your own life in order to respond in grace to those you lead. Grace-filled leadership is also truth-filled leadership. That's the dilemma we face as leaders. Not a "my way or the highway" approach to truth, but a truth that is expressed in honesty, understanding, accountability, and even love. "Who am I, O Lord God, and what have I done that You have brought me this far?" The distance God has brought you in comparison to other people isn't the point either. If you have any blessing in your life at all, the question is simple: "Who am I, Lord God, that You have brought me this far? As I confess my own weaknesses, Lord, thank You for Your grace. Allow me to lead with that same grace."

Reflections:
1. If you took the risk to consider God's grace that is offered to you, what mistakes, weaknesses, obsessions, sins, or shame are highlighted and brought into the light that make you afraid?
2. Would those you lead describe you as a grace-filled leader? Would those you lead describe you as a truth-filled leader? If you aren't sure, ask them. This conversation will not only help you become more aware, but will also give you an opportunity to express the challenge you face as a leader to be

truthful and full of grace in the very same moment. Followers understand your burden if you give them a chance.

3. Consider God's blessing in your life and say David's prayer. *O Lord God, who am I that You have provided all this for me? You have looked on me as though I were the most exalted of all. I know I am not, but I am so thankful to You. Allow me to lead with that same grace today.*

Part IV

The Question of Action: What You Must Do?

Chapter 21

Who Will Lead Next?

Leader 1:	Thanks for coming today. As you know, we've been looking to fill this position for the last six months. We were excited to meet you. You have all the right experience, and your educational background is very impressive. Can you tell us a little about why you're interested in this position?
Leader 2:	To be honest, this job fits me and will help me get to the next level. I want this job because I am successful, resourceful, productive, and this job fits with my career goals. I want this job, and I'm looking forward to being hired.
Leader 1:	You seem to want this job really bad. Are you sure you're thinking about this job? You'll be responsible for the future, work, and development of one hundred people.
Leader 2:	Oops, sorry. I thought this was the leadership position you posted.

The intentional process of selecting, developing, and training those who will be in charge after you leave, are fired, incapacitated, or die is known as succession planning. Succession planning is simply the process by which organizations think strategically about who will lead them next. If you reflect for a moment on this process, what's interesting is how little thought we give to the question of why. Why would we as today's leaders be motivated to spend our time and resources developing the next generation of leaders, or more precisely, those who will lead after we are gone?

Before we go any further, let's get grounded in reality. First, you are developing leaders to lead an organization where you may not be remembered, where everything you have done may be gone soon after you leave, and where the leader who takes your place may declare that everything you did was bad and all that is to come after you is now good. Second, once you leave you may soon be forgotten. In fairness to the leaders who will take your place, hanging around after you have left is much worse than you being forgotten. Leaders who aren't willing to let go can be such a thorn in the side of successors. The more you have invested, the more you need to let others lead when you are done. Third, despite the time you spent securing your organization's, family's, or church's financial future—or securing your vision in stone—others will have a different agenda than you. These are the succession planning realities. Still, succession planning is important. Legacy planning is planning for a world where you will never have to die and your impact will live on. Succession planning is planning for a world where you are gone, really gone. Why in the world would you plan for that?

We are responsible for developing the next generation of leaders, but why? Why are you interested in developing leaders who will lead after you are "dead" in all practical ways to the organization you have given so much of yourself to serving? One interesting way to think about succession planning is to think about what you would want to hear from a leader who is moving on to a new organization. I recently read a farewell letter from an executive that was addressed to the community of stakeholders in the organization where he served. After I read the letter I immediately felt a sense of abandonment for those he was leaving behind. What are the right things to say in such a letter? I'm not sure. What I am sure of is that this particular leader had not done all he could to develop his successor or successors. One of the reasons was that he himself was only in the position for four years prior to his leaving.

Some might argue that new leaders are too busy pushing their own agenda in the first few years to think toward their successors, but the reality is that leaders often move on to their next challenge very quickly. Where does responsibility for succession planning begin? It begins on the day you step into leadership, but it requires a selflessness that is willing to consider your organization, or your family for that matter, without you.

My wife and I have been in the process of fine tuning our will, and more specifically, considering where our kids will go if we die. It's a succession planning dilemma at its finest because we are considering who will lead our children after we are gone. We both realized that much of the conversation was about trying to control the outcomes and making sure our kids turned out just the way we would like. In defense of those family members we considered as guardians, we realized something important. In the planning, we had to consider the life and future of our children when someone else was their parent. First, we considered what would happen to our estate after our death. Would our kids get any leftover money at some predetermined age, or would control of our estate go to their new parents? Second, we had asked someone else to take responsibility for parenting our two little boys. And finally, in this pretend world we were imagining, we were now dead. Not just gone for a while, but gone from this world. Planning for the future of our kids when we know longer had any say in the way things would god was really interesting for us. In the event of our death, we wanted the best for our kids and for their new parents. Therefore, we had to answer a really important question. What can we do while we are still here to help everyone involved move forward in our absence? That's the heart of success planning.

Succession planning in organizations isn't so different from planning for your will and your children's future. Planning for your children's future in case of your absence should begin the day they are born. Not for the sake of your own security, but for the sake of your children's future. You will be gone, and they won't. Planning for your successor as a leader should begin the day you take the job. This planning isn't done for the sake of securing a future that you see, but for securing the possibility for another leader who will lead with your same courage and conviction, humility and connectedness. Succession planning shouldn't be for the sake of survival alone, but for the sake of those you lead. When we do take the time to consider developing our successors, we often think about ways to ensure that everything stays the same as it is today. We don't often think about how a successor could actually improve what we have done.

Reflection:
1. Do you develop others to take your place, or are you preparing those around you so they will know where to look for the type of leader who can lead at your level of responsibility?
2. Why do you develop others? Are you developing the next generation of leaders because you want to sustain what you have built? Are you developing the

next generation of leaders for the sake of those you
lead?

3. Have you come to the realization that planning for
   your replacement has absolutely nothing to do with
   you? If your answer is yes, then what are you doing
   to prepare others for a world without you? If your
   answer is no, how did you come to believe that a
   world without you has anything to do with you?

4. What would it take for you to prepare those you lead
   to take your job?

Chapter 22

Communicating Hope

Doctor: "I have some <u>good</u> news and some <u>bad</u> news."

Patient: "So what's the <u>good</u> news, Doc?"

Doctor: "Well, they're going to name a disease after you."

"The truth is that you will be in Babylon for seventy years. But then I will come and do for you all the good things I have promised, and I will bring you home again. For I know the plans I have for you," says the LORD. "They are plans for good and not for disaster, to give you a future and a hope. In those days when you pray, I will listen."

Jeremiah 29:10-12

I have spent the last seventeen years of my life dealing with back pain. My family and friends are aware of it, but I try not to let the pain rule my life. In fact, I often assume that everyone must live in some form of physical pain because while it hurts to sit or stand, I usually get by. For those of you who know your body parts, I have an L4 disc herniation and deteriorating facet joints in my lower back. I have never seriously pursued a surgical option to overcome my pain, but I have been through every other kind of treatment imaginable from physical therapy, to massage, to chiropractic work, to epidural injections, and finally to acupuncture. On top of that, I have sustained my lifestyle by taking between four and ten ibuprofen tablets every day for the past seventeen years.

While some of these treatments have provided relief over the years, more recently I have come to the point that the pain running from my back to the bottoms of my feet has become so intense that I am overwhelmed by its ability to drive most decisions in my life. It limits what I can do, hinders my ability to interact with my kids, and is a nagging reality for my family and friends. While I have avoided the use of narcotics to ease the pain because I know the danger of addiction to these medications, I fully understand why others use them just to get by.

While the pain has been tolerable over the years, with a couple of trips to the emergency room during periods of acute pain, the last month has put me at the end of my rope. After waking up this morning at 5a.m. unable to calm the nerve pain in my back, I realized something very important: I had finally begun to lose hope. I also realized what hope is for me and my back pain. Hope is not the possibility that I will be pain-free, but the possibility that my pain will improve, that I will get better, and that I will be able to live with a tolerable level of pain. Pain has become such a consistent part of my psyche that the thought of a pain-free life isn't on my radar. This morning, after three hours of writhing pain, immune to my changing positions or my attempts to leave my body behind in deep meditation, I became something I didn't like. I became hopeless. I had finally started to wonder if there was any hope that I would ever be free of pain. The four ibuprofen tablets finally kicked in after my stretching routine, and I was able to think a little more clearly and move into my workday. By the way, those tablets are making it possible for me to write this. At the point I was able to think again, a glimmer of hope came back to me as I called my orthopedic surgeon and general practitioner to get some advice. We'll see how this episode plays out.

While we often ask leaders to provide us with a vision and purpose for our organizations, we don't usually think of them as providing hope. Hope is the possibility of something better. As long as we are able to embrace even a glimmer of hope, we can hold out, work through the adversity, and move forward. When the possibility of something better disappears, we are hopeless and we are done.

If leaders provide us with anything, they must provide hope. Jeremiah 29:11 is often cited as the scriptural promise from God that He always provides us with a continuing hope in a better future. Reading this scripture tells us more about Jeremiah's words regarding hope in God. Jeremiah indicates that the Israelites will be captives in Babylon for seventy years, more than a lifetime for many of those who heard his words. Even though many of those hearing his words would not live to see freedom from captivity, Jeremiah goes on to proclaim God's promise that He is in control and will provide a hope and a future for His people. Jeremiah also asks God's people to go ahead and prosper in spite of their situation, and to trust in the future that God has planned for them.

To have faith in a leader is to trust in their vision for our future. To have faith as a leader who is dying to lead is to understand the challenge of the present and to maintain a hope in a future that is promised and yet to come. Hope isn't always built on the realization of all our dreams in our lifetime, but on the possibility of our dreams being lived out by other generations and in eternity. Leaders bear the responsibility for providing and communicating hope. If you lead for your own gain, then hope isn't your responsibility. But if you are attempting to understand leadership outside of yourself, being hopeful and communicating a faith in possibility is your opportunity and daily challenge. It's hardest for me when I myself feel hopeless. But I realize that I have chosen to lead, and by default, have chosen to maintain hope for those I lead.

When things are good, hope tends to be either unnecessary or focused on the idea that things will remain good. When our situations get tough and we are facing job layoffs, financial insecurity, career transitions, family tragedy, or physical pain, hope in something better is often the only thing that sustains us. Strategically then, communicating hope becomes a leader's top priority. Generating faith in that hope as a leader is difficult when you yourself are in the same space as your followers or family, but hope is that possibility. Hope is always possible and comes from our faith in things we have not seen, in risks we are willing to take, and in a step of confidence that builds more confidence.

Reflections:
1. Think of the last time you communicated hope to someone else. What is it about you that allowed you to communicate that hope?
2. How can you become more deliberate about communicating hope to those you lead? What is one thing you could do today to communicate hope to someone you lead who may be approaching hopelessness? Focus in on understanding the source of their hopelessness before communicating the possibility of a better future for them, and avoid the temptation to provide an empty statement of hope. Take confidence that oftentimes just listening to someone provides them with hope.
3. Consider God's promise to you. Where are the painful or challenging areas of your life where you need hope in a better future for yourself, your descendants, or for those you lead?
4. What is it that those you currently lead are hoping for, and what can you do today to grow or sustain that hope?

Chapter 23

Whatever It Takes

A guy shows up late for work. The boss yells,
"You should've been here at 8:30!"
The guy replies, "Why? What happened at 8:30?"

So God said to Noah, "I am going to put an end to all
people, for the earth is filled with violence because of
them. I am surely going to destroy both them and the
earth. So make yourself an ark of cypress..."

Genesis 6:13-14

B ecause of my jobs as an organizational change consultant and university professor in the same area, I'm often
asked about how change takes place in people and organizations. While there are tools and quality research to help you
find out on your own if that's a nagging question for you,
after years of studying change and trying to change myself
and the organizations I serve, I do have some suggestions.
The first suggestion is to do whatever it takes.

I like to work out. For whatever reason, working out in
the gym is a fairly disciplined part of my life. I have spent
the last two decades since my adolescent years in the gym
primarily playing basketball and lifting weights. Now in my
late thirties (ok, early forties) as of this writing, my workout
regimen is very predictable. I play basketball two times a
week for an hour and I lift weights for thirty minutes on
the three off days. Over the years, many of my friends have
asked me for advice on working out and getting on a program
to stay in shape (or get in shape). My answer is simple. Do
whatever it takes. If I had to write a book on working out at
this point in my life, that would be the title. And the chapters of the book would be simple. The chapter on getting
started would be called, "If you really want to work out,
go to the gym." The chapter on muscle building would be
called, "Lift something heavier than just your limbs." The
chapter on cardiovascular training would be titled, "Move
around until you are breathing hard." The chapter on motivation would be called, "If you get bored, try something that's
more interesting." The chapter on avoiding injury would be
called, "Stretch out and start slow." The chapter on dealing

with an injury or pain would be called, "If it hurts, don't do it and do something else." Finally, the chapter on sticking with it would be called, "If you really want the benefits of working out, keep working out."

If this all sounds silly, ridiculously obvious, or even skeptical that's because it is a little silly and obvious, and I am a bit of a skeptic. I would also have to open such a book with the caveat that I'm no trainer or physical therapist and that this is just what has worked for me. However, if you think about it, there's a lot of truth to these ideas. The bottom line is this. Nothing is going to change until you really want it to change badly enough, and you have to face the obvious. When you are truly ready to do something different, whatever it takes will probably work.

When I meet with leaders who may engage me as a consultant to their organizations I try to make one thing clear. Nothing is going to change unless they really want to see change. If those in power aren't looking for change, then nothing big will change. If the time for something different has arrived and they want to do anything except what they are currently doing, then almost any change process or consultant will work. The worst thing you can do as a leader is talk about change when you really aren't committed to changing anything. And being willing to change things has to start with you as the leader. The organization you lead probably won't change a bit unless you are willing to change your leadership, your perspective, or your attitude. In other words, if you want things to improve, you have to do whatever it takes to be different and to do things differently. If you aren't willing to put your own current way of being on the table as the first sacrifice, don't patronize those you lead by talking about organizational change. It's just not very interesting.

The second change strategy has to do with how to make the first step toward change. Along with working out in the gym, I'm also a musician. Over the years, I have had several friends ask me how to learn to play guitar. My advice has now become very simple. If you want to learn to play guitar, set a date two months out where you will have to play for other people you don't know. This might include leading songs for your church's youth group or playing at an open mic night at your local coffee shop. Whatever the venue, set a concert date and tell as many people as you can about it so you really can't get out of it without feeling like a complete schmuck.

In my experience, people who buy a guitar, take lessons, or buy the latest "learning guitar" DVD rarely practice for more than a few weeks. For those who set a date to perform or lead with a guitar, the learning curve is steep and motivating. It often works because something is now on the line for them. For the new musician, commitment to perform music or lead others with music puts so much on the line. For some reason, playing music and the way others perceive our talent creates a great deal of personal pressure. Playing music when you haven't mastered the skill, or when you still think those who don't play will be able to tell the difference, puts our egos, our identity, and all that makes us comfortable right on the line. If you want to learn to play guitar, set a high-profile concert date.

If setting deadlines at work is easy for you and you think that setting a high-profile date is also easy, you may be missing the point. Many people are good at setting deadlines and getting things done. However, those who have come to the point where they really want things to change set high-profile dates to perform or deliver in areas where they are truly on the edge of themselves, their confidence, and their skill. If you want to change yourself and your organization, you have to be willing to make a high-profile commitment to changes that will make you just as uncomfortable as it will those you lead. That's the difference. If you truly want things to be different, make a high-profile, time-specific commit-ment to the change, and be sure the commitment makes you feel a bit uncomfortable. If it doesn't, it may mean you are suggesting change for others without any commitment to actually change yourself. For some of us, being in a different place tomorrow requires a commitment to a high-profile action that stretches us. Rehearsal or repeated words without a reason for rehearsing usually doesn't get you there on its own.

Most of us are familiar with the story of Noah, the flood, and the ark. However, have you ever considered all that was at stake for Noah? Noah had a family, a connection to his family, and by all accounts had lived a righteous life before God. Then God set a very high-impact and high-profile date in front of Noah. Although Noah certainly had the opportu-nity to disobey, the pressure of the date and the urgency of the impending flood provided Noah with the motivation to do and be something different, and for that matter, to learn a new skill. He learned to build a very large boat in no time at all. If you are tempted to dismiss Noah's concern about what other people thought because he knew they were all going to perish, you are overestimating the human mind's ability to see past the pressure of the present. Noah had to build an ark with everyone around watching the madness. In addition, there is every indication that as Noah dragged his family into the ark building process with him, he was as close to the edge of his own comfort zone as any of his family or followers. The sacrifice necessary for Noah to complete this task had to be tremendous, and it caused him to do whatever it took to get the job done.

Reflections:

1. What change are you considering for yourself, your team, or your organization? On a scale from 1 to 10 (1 being very comfortable and 10 being completely

on the edge), rate how much this change puts you on the edge of your comfort zone.

2. Thinking of this same change, on a scale from 1 to 10 (1 being very comfortable and 10 being completely on the edge), rate how much this change puts your followers on the edge of their comfort zones.

3. Subtract the number you calculated for others from the number you calculated for yourself. If the number is not a zero or a positive number, consider the fact that you are asking others to be or do something that you yourself are not willing to be or do. What are you not willing to sacrifice that you are asking others to sacrifice?

4. What change are you considering for your family? On a scale from 1 to 10 (1 being very comfortable and 10 being completely on the edge), rate how much this change puts you on the edge of your comfort zone.

Chapter 24

Shut Up!

"The most interesting information comes from children, for they tell all they know and then stop."
                                                        - Mark Twain

He who answers before listening—that is his folly
and his shame.

Proverbs 18:13

Have you ever been part of a conversation with someone
else and realized midway that you haven't been saying
a word while the other person has done all the talking? I
certainly have, and oftentimes during these conversations
a voice screams out inside my head, "Hey, I'm bored, not
saying anything, and this person has no idea!" Even more
disturbingly, I have also been the person who won't shut up.
I have caused others to make the same statement inside their
own heads. I know this because I have a few people close to
me who have let me know.

For many, listening is an incredible challenge. We speak
for a variety of reasons. In some cases we speak because
our voice, our convictions, our thoughts, and our feelings
should be heard and need to be heard. In other cases, we
speak because we are angry and reactive and our voice is a
way to lash back at others. In still other cases we speak out
of anxiety or a fear of silence. If there is silence, we will fill
it with our voice. The silence highlights the loud voice in our
own head that wants to speak on behalf of us, often at the
expense of the more thoughtful and less vocal people around
us. If you have ever been accused of being a poor listener
with a loud voice, the advice is simple. Have the courage to
shut up.

As a leader, your voice matters. What matters to you and
how you communicate that gives your followers a confidence in your vision and your ability to provide clarity and
purpose to their work. Best of all, they know what to expect
from you because you often tell them. However, that's only
part of what your leadership means. Your voice is necessary
to the job of leading in all areas of your life, at work and
at home. But it isn't enough. In fact, as your responsibility

grows it will become increasingly difficult to lead well if you rely too heavily upon any one of these strengths. In a world full of organizations that celebrate high performance, self-centeredness, and achievement as the most important thing, what does it take to stay connected to those around you.

As your successes add up, your business grows, and you get more pressure to move forward—to produce and to build a body of accomplishments—oftentimes your ability and willingness to hear others is damaged. Others know immediately that you no longer value their input. In fact, you might think and say that you value the input of others, but the pressure to do more and do it well completely mutes your ability to stay in touch. So what is a leader to do? Realize that your ability to stay connected and to slow down and hear the voices of your stakeholders, your team, and your family are key to your ability to truly lead well. You cannot lead well without their input, but you will face increasing pressure to do otherwise.

In any conversation, make a mental note of the amount of time your spend hearing versus the amount of time you spend talking. Be careful here, because we often confuse hearing with relating. The problem with relating your experience to the experience someone else is having is that it often sabotages your ability to hear. Ask questions about their story. To hear is to avoid the temptation to turn their story into your story. To hear is to stay on track with what they are saying and not make it about you. You might say, "But I like to relate to people, and I need to help them understand that I've been through their experience." Stop it! I'm not concerned that you'll stop relating. That's your gift. Your trouble is hearing. So let them tell their story completely without making it about you in any way. There will be time for you to tell your story later.

What does it mean to be a good listener? When you think of those in your life you consider good listeners, what is it that makes them good listeners? Here are some ideas. When you are in conversation with others, do you choose to speak or just speak? Good listeners either are just naturally good at listening, or they choose when to speak as opposed to speaking because they just do. If you are a talker, good listening involves a conversation in your own head about when to insert your own voice into a conversation. If there is no conversation going on in your own head, there probably isn't a conversation going on outside of your head either.

Next, get comfortable with silence. In conversation with your team members, shut up long enough to let them think and speak in two different moments. Stop talking as a way to make yourself more comfortable in conversation. We often miss the truly important thoughts of others because we aren't comfortable letting them sit with their thoughts before they speak, even for a few moments.

Finally, communicate passionately about the importance of the first two points made above. You not only need to model this way of being, you must let your team know that the ability to hear is a core competency they must develop.

Reflections:
1. Are you a good listener? If you said yes, ask yourself how you know that. Do you know because others tell you that you are, or because you just assume you are? If you said no, then consider that you might be better than you think or consider asking those you lead about your listening. What would help them to feel heard?
2. When other people speak to you, are you trying to understand what they are saying or constantly formulating your own opinions about what they are saying? If you have difficulty staying connected to the stories of others, you may be missing out. Next time you feel yourself wanting to provide the answers for others

or make their story your story, avoid the temptation. If you can't stay on track in conversation, then try not saying anything at all. Another option is to find a trusted friend and practice listening, staying with their story, and paraphrasing their story back to them until you understand them better.

3. Do you spend time in silence when you pray? Complete silence even from the voices in your head? Commit to praying every day for the next week without saying or thinking a word. It will be difficult, but keep trying and allow yourself to be frustrated to the point that you begin to be comfortable in real silence. Watch what happens.

Chapter 25

Throwing Yourself
Under the Bus

How many narcissists does it take
to change a lightbulb?

Just one...

Hold onto the lightbulb and the whole world
revolves around you.

Above his head they placed the written charge against him: THIS IS JESUS, THE KING OF THE JEWS. Two robbers were crucified with him, one on his right and one on his left. Those who passed by hurled insults at him, shaking their heads and saying, "You who are going to destroy the temple and build it in three days, save yourself! Come down from the cross, if you are the Son of God!"

In the same way the chief priests, the teachers of the law and the elders mocked him. "He saved others," they said, "but he can't save himself! He's the King of Israel! Let him come down now from the cross, and we will believe in him. He trusts in God. Let God rescue him now if he wants him, for he said, 'I am the Son of God.'" In the same way the robbers who were crucified with him also heaped insults on him.

Matthew 27:37-44

About a week ago my wife and I got into a pretty heated argument. We've been married for ten years this summer, and so this wasn't our first argument, nor will it be our last. As usual, as the "discussion" went on, our egos began to take their corners and we both buckled down for what promised to be a solid, intentional, and energetic battle of wills. Then, like a cold bucket of water on my head, I saw my wife do something she has probably done many times, but it had never been quite so obvious to me. She threw herself under the bus. I don't think she had any idea that I was aware of it, but that's exactly what she did. I saw a switch in her approach to our fight that was an obvious choice to let her self-centered defenses down, refuse to attack back, and seek out mutual understanding. Now keep in mind that she was doing this at a time when I had made no such choice, with my own self-centered defenses up and at the ready. But without any explanation for this tactic and fully knowing she would get no credit for this surrender, she took one for the team, she surrendered her will for the good of the family, and she did it alone. There was a very good chance I may not even notice, but on this particular occasion I did. In fact, I remember thinking to myself, *She just threw herself under the bus! For the sake of what?*

Because I know my wife, I also realized that this was probably one of many times she had done this, making a conscious choice to put her will aside for the sake of me, for our kids, or maybe for all of us. Whatever the case, it highlights something important about leaders who are dying to lead. Leading well often requires you to throw yourself under the bus, to take a hit either from or for the team that you are likely never to get credit for, be able to explain, or even understand yourself. I have had conversation after conversation with people in every level of leadership about this, and one thing is certain. Leaders who understand what is at stake and are able to lead for the sake of others have to stuff many things away in places where no one will ever know. Executives have to make decisions about how money will be spent every day, and because the interests of those they lead are all over the map, the leader is forced to make the best decision possible, often in situations where the reasoning will never make sense to everyone. Board members and CEOs withhold information regarding poor decisions of vice presidents in order to protect the livelihood and reputation of people who made just a single mistake. Managers having to lay off their teams keep information to themselves that they are legally unable to share, while their team members are buying homes and cars, never knowing that the layoff is just around the corner.

Before you judge these individuals for these decisions, keep in mind that the more leadership responsibility you have, the more inherent tensions you will face. Multiple stakeholders will want many things, and many things that are in direct contradiction to one another. This is not to say the leaders don't face clearly defined situations every day where public reporting is necessary and the answers are, or should be, clear. But unless you are operating in the leadership role, you may never completely understand what it's like to live in that sort of world. It can be a lonely world for these leaders. Former peers who were friends won't understand your new leadership role when you become their boss. Sacrificial leadership means dying to the very part of you that not only wants to defend yourself, but wants others to understand every decision you make and every time you throw yourself under the bus.

If anyone had a right to defend Himself, to explain the reasons for His actions in His darkest hour, it was Jesus Christ as He hung on the cross. I feel so ill-prepared to discuss the loneliness He must have felt when everyone around Him was telling Him to defend Himself, to show His power, and to remove Himself from that painful and humiliating position. Most of the time, when I feel challenged, pressured, or taunted, I want to bite back at others and let them have it. But instead, Jesus chose to obey His calling. They knew He made some strong statements about God's ultimate power, but He chose obedience for the sake of the world, and for you and me. We didn't deserve it. He understood that. But even so, He chose death over self-preservation. He chose love over hatred. He chose obedience over Himself. He chose a lonely death for the sake of a guilty world over a triumphant victory of lightning bolts, vengeful statements, and setting those blind fools in their places.

As you read this, you may be thinking of a leader who has made these kinds of choices. This is probably someone you have reported to, known as a mentor, read about, had as a peer, or have been married to. This is probably a person who takes very little credit, works hard for the sake of others, and will probably never show up in a book about leadership, because no one will know. But a handful of people, including you, do know. You understand the sacrificial nature of that leader's character. You saw it play out on multiple occasions and possibly over multiple years. What would it take for you to become that kind of leader?

I know a person like this. I reported to him for years. If he read this, he wouldn't even realize it was him I was describing. That's the point. He's not looking for credit. He's looking to serve others and to serve faithfully. My leader isn't weak. He's strong. He has powerful convictions and beliefs. The key is that his convictions rarely just include him. I would like to be him, but I often fall short. I know my leader often makes decisions, tough decisions, alone. I know he takes heat I don't realize he takes. But in him I see, inasmuch as possible from another human being, someone who expresses the strength of character that Jesus expressed on the cross. What a gift he has been to me.

Reflections:
1. Can you identify a leader you know who has thrown him or herself under the bus on multiple occasions or even possibly for you? Have you thanked them for who they are and for their leadership in your life?
2. It was once said that you are who surrounds you. Do those around you encourage you to sacrifice yourself for the Christ's sake or for the sake of those in need around you? Or, are you surrounded by people who focus on saving themselves at all costs?
3. How can you encourage others to lead this way? When it comes to the team, family members, or organization where you lead, how can you create an environment where leaders are appreciated for their service to others?

Chapter 26

Looking for Character?

Actual quotes taken from job performance reviews:

"I would not allow this employee to breed."
"He would be out of his depth in a
parking lot puddle."
"This employee is depriving a village
somewhere of an idiot."
"This employee should go far, and the
sooner he starts, the better."
"Got into the gene pool when the lifeguard
wasn't watching."
"Got a full six-pack, but lacks the plastic
thingy to hold it together."
"A gross ignoramus - 144 times worse than
an ordinary ignoramus."

W ould those for whom you are accountable define you as a leader of character? When I ask myself that question, I have to hesitate for a moment. To suggest that others might identify me as a person of character is such an attractive and intimidating thought. While I can easily imagine that those I lead might say I mean well, I'm not sure they would name *character* as a trait that comes to mind first when they think of my leadership. However, I sure wish they would. For me, to be defined as a leader of character would mean that although not everyone likes me, most of my followers respect me, trust me, and see depth and discernment in me.

We often don't know how to get at character because we don't give ourselves permission to ask questions that really matter. I recently had the opportunity to hear one of the world's most renowned researchers and consultants speak on the topic of leadership. He has worked with leaders at the highest levels of government around the world and has helped many Fortune 100 companies select their top leaders. He told amazing stories and certainly identified some critical elements of effective leadership. After his presentation, the audience barraged him with questions regarding his experience working with leaders. After several questions had been discussed, a guy in the back row of the auditorium asked him, "Based on your experiences and research on leadership, how would you define character, and how do you interview for character?" What a great question. Keep in mind that this question was being raised at a time when several top corporate leaders had been removed and others were standing trial for bad decision-making. I was on the edge of my seat, curious for an answer that would help us select better leaders in the future. I'll never forget the response. The expert said, "I'm going to duck that question and respond with a story." After a story about a historical leader, he still hadn't defined character and didn't get to the second question, how do you interview for it?

If you think about the leaders who have fallen in the last several years, almost all of them had the experiences and resumes that would indicate they could do their jobs. Many had the competencies, skills, and relationships needed to succeed. With all this evidence, they would have looked like high-potential leaders on a succession plan for the jobs they finally occupied in the very significant businesses where they worked. But, in so many cases, none of this mattered. Many leaders make very poor choices. Affairs with co-workers, tax evasion, siphoning millions of dollars out of corporate coffers for their own gain, breaking of company policies—these are just a few of the bad decisions out there. At the core of each of their problems was a significant flaw that was overlooked, either because it couldn't be seen, it was ignored, or no one knew where to look when they interviewed these leaders.

It's helpful to think of character as the continual imprinting on your life that comes from words you remember from others, statements about you that have forever changed your self-perception, the mark of crucible-type experiences that have shaped you, your family history and legacy, and God's voice into your life. Your character is an imprint that you carry into every conversation and relationship in your life, and that matters because character is all about relationships. The way you show up in relationship to your friends, spouse, parents, children, co-workers, boss, and with the guy who cuts you off on the freeway shows your imprint. But that imprint develops slowly and takes time both [AU: do you mean "to print" here?] print and to be changed. Your character drives your worldview, and your worldview impacts everything.

If the imprint on your life has been to make everything about you, you may be seen as someone who is trying to convince everyone else that you are good enough. The big problem with this is that you aren't good enough. In fact, much of the time you aren't good at all. At our wedding, my wife and I invited a close friend to read some Scripture and say a few words. After he read a Bible verse he said, "The vows that you are about to say, you cannot keep." At that, the entire church went silent, including my wife and me. Then he went on to say, "It is only by the grace of God that you will be able to be faithful, loving, and committed to each other until death."

Those words didn't make much sense to me then, but today, after ten years of marriage, they make perfect sense. We are all capable to letting people down, and it's not because we may do bad things, but because we all *will* do bad things and make bad choices. That's a very different approach to what it means to have character. To be a person of character is to be aware of your nature to make everything about you, at the expense of others. To confess your need for the grace of God and the grace of others—and to offer grace to others—is the first step. But it takes an awareness and confession of your limitations and your sin.

When it comes to hiring leaders, how can we increase the probability of selecting the right leaders for the right jobs? Might character have something to do with it? There is little doubt that character matters, but how do we interview for it? And how do we look for it when the pressure for results often comes first, with character ending up on the list as a "nice to have" quality? For those interested in making character a "must have" quality for leaders, your next step will be to clearly define what character is, and how you will further develop it in yourself and in those you lead.

Next time you think about your own leadership or interview someone else, consider these things. Are you resilient, and have you persevered through long times of suffering and challenge? How have you dealt with challenges? Were you overcome by the situation, did you blame others for your circumstances, or did you focus on what you could control? Do you avoid pandering to the powerful, move forward with a healthy sense of your own strengths and limitations, and avoid the temptation to make everything about you? Are you humbled by the high character represented in others? Are you able to maintain yourself in times of pressure and challenge, regulating what you feel and continuing to take in new information? Do you focus on what could be as opposed to what isn't? Do you communicate a genuine and deep concern and love for others? Are you willing and able to communicate your deepest convictions? Do others trust you to keep information shared between you and them? And finally, are you a person who spends a significant amount of time developing yourself, reflecting on behaviors and perspectives that might need changing?

By the way, people of character rarely label themselves as people of character. The irony is that their character probably won't allow it. Be wary of leaders who identify themselves as people of character. An overconfidence in our own ability to exude and portray character could indicate a disconnect regarding the real sacrifice necessary to follow Christ. Leaders who lead with character just live it and are always in touch with their inability to save themselves. A leader who is dying to lead has come to grips with his or her inability to get there on their own.

Reflections:

1. What are two actions you could take today that would get one or two of your followers to say, "Wow, I really respect the fact that (you) did that today?"

2. Think of a situation where you felt personal pressure from others as a leader, pressure because they didn't agree with you, like you, respect you, or understand you? What did others contribute to the situation? What did you contribute to the situation? If you can't think of a situation like this, watch out—more reflection is needed. All leaders have had these experi-

ences. Are you willing and able to see how you really lead, how others react to you, and what you should have done better?].

3. Who are the people in your life to whom you owe an apology? As you think about apologizing to them, make sure it's not just so you feel better, but because you need to apologize. Be aware that some apologies are completely selfish. For some people in your life who may not know you anymore, an apology could drag up too much history to be helpful. At the very least, make the confession to God.

4. What matters most to you? If you say work, dig deeper. If you follow up with family, dig deeper. If family matters most to you, how does that impact how you live *and* work? If you say your relationship with God, how is your relationship with God reflected in your leadership? Where is God still working with you?

Chapter 27

Givers and Takers

Therapist:	"Maybe you should take some time to consider what you contributed to the failure of your marriage."
Patient:	"What do you mean when you say, what I contributed?"
Therapist:	"I mean, what do you need to take responsibility for, what did you do wrong, and what would you do differently next time?"
Patient:	"That's a good question. Let me think about that for a second."
Therapist:	"Okay, good, let me know when you're ready."
Patient:	"I've got it! I'm too good a person and I care too much, I loved him too much, and I won't make that mistake in my next marriage."

As a human being you have many choices every day of your life. You will have to choose whether to wake up this morning or stay in bed, to lead others or be a follower, to eat three meals or skip one or two, to focus on God's agenda or follow your own agenda, to serve or be served. One of the biggest choices you will have to make is whether you will be a giver or a taker today. It's no secret that life is full of giving and taking. But let's be clear about one thing: we're not talking about giving and receiving, we're talking about giving and taking. At certain times, all of us have to be receivers of help from others. In fact, it is a necessary part of our organizational and community life together. But some of us are just takers.

Takers are people who have no problem making everything about them. They ask for help when they don't need it. They feel entitled to take because they are just too busy to give back, at least right now. They need to feel in control, smart, and served by others. They feel little guilt about their taking because they are just so overwhelmed by life and what life owes them that they are due their share. They control the outcomes because ultimately they want their own needs to be served. Takers may serve in significant leadership roles in organizations built largely of givers, but the leaders themselves may be takers from those in their own organization. Takers are often control freaks who feel a need to control everything, in spite of the fact that their inability to let go is making life miserable for everyone else.

Givers are another story. You know givers. My mother-in-law is a giver. When she asks you a question she isn't looking for the answer she wants to hear. When she offers help, it is out of a sincere desire to help. When she plays with her grandkids, she is interested in giving them something, not making them be or become something that will make her feel better. She just gives. Givers have little need to make life about them. They ask you questions and really want to hear your answers. Givers are interested in you, often at the expense of their own time and resources. Givers often don't think of themselves as givers because if they did, they would be takers. That's the irony.

The fact is that most of us fall somewhere between the two. However, we all have the potential to become takers. Leaders who are takers are dangerous to follow because they don't think about the whole system, they just think, *How will this impact me?* Takers are rewarded in many organizations because they can be strong drivers for results, but they will put results above the needs of anyone else around them. The taker in each of us keeps us from seeing the opportunities to make a difference in the lives of others that surround us every day. For many leaders in large businesses, giving and taking often comes down to daily decisions about how to spend their time. Will I spend a good portion of my time developing others in my business, even though I know that same time spent on getting business results will get me to a quick promotion? I'm not making the argument that developing other people is bad for your business; in fact it's good. But the tension to focus on you, your network, and credit for the things your team is doing is the reality for leaders.

Reflections:
1. If you were leaving your organization tomorrow, would there be at least two people you had prepared for the challenge of occupying your job?
2. What is keeping you from spending time developing the leadership capacity in those you lead?
3. What are three habits you can put in place right now to make sure that those you lead are being stretched, developed, and engaged in their work?

Chapter 28

What Do You Want?

"Do you have trouble making up your mind?
Well, yes or no?"

The king said to me, "What is it you want?"

Then I prayed to the God of heaven, and I answered the king, "If it pleases the king and if your servant has found favor in his sight, let him send me to the city in Judah where my fathers are buried so that I can rebuild it."

Then the king, with the queen sitting beside him, asked me, "How long will your journey take, and when will you get back?" It pleased the king to send me; so I set a time.

I also said to him, "If it pleases the king, may I have letters to the governors of Trans-Euphrates, so that they will provide me safe-conduct until I arrive in Judah? And may I have a letter to Asaph, keeper of the king's forest, so he will give me timber to make beams for the gates of the citadel by the temple and for the city wall and for the residence I will occupy?" And because the gracious hand of my God was upon me, the king granted my requests.

Nehemiah 2:4-8

I recently sat with a colleague of mine who was struggling with the challenge of motivating her team in the midst of adverse times. Her team was losing many battles and beginning to blame her for the outcome. In fact, the team had begun to meet behind her back to talk about certain leadership issues that had emerged. After hearing her talk through the situation, I came to the conclusion that at least two things were going on. First, her team was looking for someone to blame for their own sense of defeat, and their insecurities and lack of self-awareness were merely feeding the flames that had brought them a sense of defeat in the first place. And second, this particular leader had not yet communicated with her group from her gut.

While she was a talented technical leader and was always acutely aware of what needed to be fixed, she had not yet communicated what she really wanted for them. When I asked her to identify the two things she wanted her team to be about, she identified two very respectful goals. First, she wanted her team members to always communicate up as opposed to sideways or down. In other words, don't gossip with your peers or subordinates. And second, she wanted the members of the group to build respect for one another. I told her that while these goals were noble, they did anything but inspire me. I knew that what she wanted for her team was much deeper than that, and her vision was tied to some things that would make her vulnerable to her team like never before.

I asked her again, What is it that you want for your team deep inside your gut, and why do you want that? I told her my own story of times when I had communicated from my gut and the way people had responded. After hearing my story she said with tears in her eyes, "I put this team together from scratch. As a leader, this is the first time I can actually say that I built this team. I'm a new leader in this organiza-tion, and I want them to succeed so badly. But at the same time, I'm so afraid. I'm afraid that I don't have the compe-tence and character to lead them, so it's making it difficult for me to communicate that."

Nehemiah is a great example of someone who was fully aware of his need for God, and also willing to tell it like it is. In the beginning of the book of Nehemiah we see a man who confesses before God multiple times and lays his life before Him. But when it comes time to approach the king of Persia so that he can go and rebuild the wall of Jerusalem, he doesn't hesitate to tell the king exactly what he wants and what he will need to get the job done. He also doesn't over-spiritualize the message to the king. He doesn't say, "God has told me to go rebuild the wall in Jerusalem," even though he may have felt that way. He tells the king what he wants.

You know what? There is nothing that others will follow more than what is deep within your core. But you first have to spend some time in prayer and reflection on what it is you really want. So many people in leadership roles, whether parents or managers, fail to think about what they want and communicate it to those involved. It does take time, but it makes all your intentions clear, and if nothing else, your convictions will be clear. As long as what you want is connected to your followers and has their interests as its center, you can never go wrong communicating the emotion, conviction, and passion of what you see as the possibility for those who follow you.

However, being willing to be vulnerable is itself an incredible challenge for leaders. Sharing vulnerability, weaknesses, and limitations is often discouraged. It is not discouraged openly, but discouraged by the reward systems that surround us. The most obvious example is the answer provided by interviewees to the question, What is your greatest weakness? If you have ever been asked that in an interview, you probably felt the temptation to turn a weakness into a strength, or a liability into an asset. All of us have regrets, weaknesses, developmental challenges, and a history of mistakes and wrong turns. These turns and characteristics aren't always fun when exposed, but they make us human and approachable, and they provide a model of that same vulnerability for others. Expressing what you really want requires conviction and courage, but also the leap of faith that your true self will stand on its own.

Reflection:
1. When you think of your current leadership challenges at home or at work, what is it you want and

why do you want it? If what you say doesn't get you choked up or red with passion, start over. There is something within you that you need to communicate. Keep digging and asking the question until it gets to your core. What is it you want and why do you want it?

2. Is your purpose clear to those you lead? How will you know?

Chapter 29

Reclaiming Vocation

A nun at a Catholic school asks her students what
they are called to be when they grow up.
Little Suzy declares, "I'm called to be a prostitute."
"What did you say?" asks the nun, totally shocked.
"I said I'm called to be a prostitute," Suzy repeats.
"Oh, thank heavens," says the nun.
"I thought you said 'a Protestant!'"

As Jesus was walking beside the Sea of Galilee, he saw two brothers, Simon called Peter and his brother Andrew. They were casting a net into the lake, for they were fishermen. "Come, follow me," Jesus said, "and I will make you fishers of men." At once they left their nets and followed him.

Matthew 4:18-20

Have enough conversations with enough leaders and you will discover that we all approach work differently. For some, work is a means to providing them with either the financial or occupational gains they seek, or the means to allow them to serve the world in ways they truly enjoy. For others, work is their toil, their lot, and something they simply must do. There are also those who see their work as providing them with joy,] because they sincerely love what they do. As it has been said, they would do their work even if we didn't pay them. Others identify work as purposeful. Love it or hate it, they work because they see a reason behind their work that is attractive to them. Still others ask for more from work because they perceive it as their vocation and calling in life. They feel that God or an inner voice has called them to their specific work at this particular time. They believe that the serendipitous and/or providential circumstances that surrounded them provided a clear pathway to their calling. Without denying that possibility, I often wonder if these people would have followed that same calling if the pieces hadn't come together and if following that calling came with significant struggle and personal cost. In other words, would they have felt their calling so clearly if the path to it were nearly impossible to follow?

Whatever your approach to your work, one thing is interesting to point out. In our modern Western culture, we feel entitled to work that provides something good, noble, or valuable to us. For the first time in many centuries, we assume that our vocation or calling is there to bring meaning to our lives. While I would be the last to argue that joy, gladness, meaning, and personal gain are meaningless benefits or even goals of work, does calling in work always imply that there is something in it for us?

Here's what I do know. You spend anywhere from 40 to 80 hours of every 168 hours a week at work. Take away 8 hours of sleep each night and you are down to 40 to 80 hours out of every 112 hours each week you spend at work. With the onset of the virtual workspace allowing us to work from anywhere and at any time, the ratio of work to other things gets even larger as you begin to de-compartmentalize your time at work from your time at home.

You don't have to buy into the idea that who you are at work matters, but it may be a shame if you don't. The statement we often hear from leaders in defense of their actions at work is, "Hey, business is business." As if we get a free pass to be selfish and pursue self-centered or organizational-centered outcomes because we're in the business box during the week. That argument highlights a very important point. Business is a powerful concept in Western culture in the twenty-first century. It is such a powerful concept that we are somehow excused from all other pursuits for the sake of "the business." We have created noble ways to defend this way of thinking including increasing value for shareholders and employees, retaining jobs for people, and the added benefit to the economy if we are making money. While there may be nothing wrong with these goals, business has become a powerful cultural phenomenon that overwhelms and cancels out all other priorities when it is being conducted.

Because of the seductive power of business and success, it isn't surprising that the calling and commitment suggested by Jesus would create the need for a logical compartmentalization of life and work. Therein lies the fallacy in the logic that business comes first when it is being conducted. It doesn't make sense to compartmentalize our actions at work from our actions in the rest of life if we assume that Jesus wants all of us. Work is a part of life and life is a part of work. When Jesus called His disciples, He didn't say come and follow Me and I will make you fishers of men Monday to Friday, between 8 a.m. and 5 p.m. The question may not be what should work provide me, but what am I being and doing while I'm there that is in line with Christ's calling on my life. If my two boys are upstairs playing with toys and I call them to dinner, their priority to play doesn't erase the reality that my call is there. It is only an indicator of whether or not they choose to pay attention.

Dietrich Bonhoeffer, in his book *The Cost of Discipleship,* describes our calling this way:

> Because Jesus is the Christ, he has the authority to call to and demand obedience to his word. Jesus summons men to follow him not as a teacher or a pattern of the good life, but as the Christ, the Son of God. In this short text Jesus Christ and his claim are proclaimed to men. Not a word of praise is given to the disciple for his decision for Christ. We are not expected to contemplate the disciple, but only him who calls, and his absolute authority. According to our text, there is no road to faith or discipleship, no other road – only obedience to the call of Jesus.[7]

Whether you believe God has called you to your current work, your calling is being fulfilled after hours, or that God does or does not call people to specific things, one question is important for you to answer. Do you believe that Jesus Christ wants all of you or just part of you, and at times when it's convenient for you to lead for His sake? While your specific work may or may not matter to God, who you are in the lives of those you lead certainly does. You have been called to a renewed life, to a life of personal sacrifice, and to be willing to lay down your nets if Jesus asked. If you have kept your business in perspective, sacrificing it may not be an issue for you. Your vocation is a calling from God to courageously sacrifice every selfish part of you for the sake of God's kingdom. It means obedience to a new way of being. If you have placed your business ahead of God, you have made it nearly impossible to hear God's calling. He's calling you to the dinner table. Are you listening?

Reflection:

1. If you surrendered all of your life and work to God, what are you most afraid He would have you lay down for the sake of His call? Why are you afraid to lay those particular things down in order to follow Christ?
2. What opportunities would await you if you surrendered your work to God?

Chapter 30

Puking

Three ironies of authenticity:

1. The more you want to be seen as genuine, the less genuine you become.

2. The more you tell people that you're a good person, the less they'll believe you.

3. If you want to know how humble I am, just ask me.

But we have this treasure in jars of clay to show that this all-surpassing power is from God and not from us. We are hard pressed on every side, but not crushed; perplexed, but not in despair; persecuted, but not abandoned; struck down, but not destroyed. We always carry around in our body the death of Jesus, so that the life of Jesus may also be revealed in our body. For we who are alive are always being given over to death for Jesus' sake, so that his life may be revealed in our mortal body. So then, death is at work in us, but life is at work in you.

2 Corinthians 4:7-12

When we think of leaders we admire, another characteristic that comes to mind is authenticity, or genuineness. We want leaders who are steadfast, vulnerable, and open to us. We want leaders who aren't hiding behind their title, their fears, or their responsibilities. We want leaders who are present with us, pull our own real selves out, and demand that others are real with them. We want leaders who are who they seem to be, understand themselves, and won't judge us for our shortcomings as they see their own shortcomings as clearly as we see ours. We want leaders like this, but we don't always get them. Even more importantly, we aren't always this kind of leader ourselves.

I have a friend who worked in radio broadcasting for several years. We would laugh when he used his radio voice to describe everyday events. You know the voice. It's the voice on the radio that tells you about traffic jams on the I-5 freeway or about the icy roads north of the city that are causing a backup for three miles. It's the voice known in radio as the "puking voice." I'm not sure where the label comes from, but I know it when I hear it. I have often wondered if news anchors speak to their spouses and children in the same voice they use when they are on television. It's a voice that runs from deep within their gut, almost as if something is caught down there, and it's a voice that professes with supposed confidence and impartiality. Some leaders use this voice. It's not their real voice. It's not the voice they would use when they are hurt, unsure, vulnerable, or defeated. It's the voice they use to project something and to make others feel something. It's the leadership puking voice, and it is often an act.

Several years ago I felt an urging from within–a calling from God—to dig deep into leadership authenticity or genuineness. I knew I was drawn to leaders who were willing and able to be "real" with me, but I wasn't sure what I meant when I labeled them that way. My drive for genuine relationships eventually showed itself in my own work as I sought to create space for my students, my team, and my clients to be real with one another. It became so deliberate that ever since that time ten years ago, I have started every class and every conversation with a potential hire with a speech about people bringing their complete selves to the jobs and their classroom experience. In many cases I would read them a passage of Scripture from 2 Corinthians where the apostle Paul describes our lives and the containers of our treasures as "jars of clay" or cracked pots. This realization that we are imperfect, trying to figure it out, and ultimately cracked pots does something in the lives of others. It creates the potential for vulnerability in all of us. And you know what? It doesn't take a rocket scientist to figure out that vulnerability and realness are important, but really hard to *live* on a daily basis.

While it made sense and was attractive to many people I interacted with, I have since discovered that those little speeches often translated into work and classroom cultures that demanded authenticity at all costs. Students and employees alike began to see the need for something different in their experience of one another. They began to demand real interactions, where people could bring their strengths, convictions, brokenness, victories and defeats, joys and sorrows all to the same experience in a way that each person was comfortable with. While I had no idea what the outcome would be, my weak attempt at asking people to bring themselves fully to their work and learning created cultures that demanded they show up in all their glory and defeat.

I now realize I was pursuing humility at the cost of our egos. Much of our challenge is making our lives and our leadership a little less about us, and a little more about others. This is not to suggest we hang our weaknesses, sins, and faults out there on the line all the time. That could begin to feel a bit needy, annoying, and potentially even disingenuous. What I am suggesting is that you enter into a genuine conversation with those you lead, showing them your strengths as well as your limitations and insecurities. From what I have seen, those around you will add vulnerability to your list of strengths. Not vulnerability for the sake of pity, but vulnerability for the sake of being a real person, and not just their manager.

Those you lead will connect with you because of your willingness to be your imperfect self with them. Letting go of the act is difficult. We are expected to express confidence at times that we don't fully have it. But letting go of the act will produce the possibility for others to be courageous enough to be real with you. What are we really afraid of when we use our own leadership puking voice? Let go of the act. You are not perfect and everybody knows it anyway.

Reflections:
1. What are two things about you in which you feel very secure? In other words, what are two things that you know are strengths you bring as a leader...and you know they are strengths because others you trust have suggested to you that they are strengths.

2. What are two of your deep insecurities, things you would be very uncomfortable telling those you lead? What would it take for you to share one of these weaknesses with those you lead? What if you opened the door for a *real* conversation with your people that would encourage them to be themselves, to learn and grow with you, and to share some of their wishes, insecurities, lost opportunities, and achieved potential? You might be saying, "I can't do that." Why not? As you answer the question of why not, consider whether your reasoning is good enough to avoid having a real and vulnerable conversation with those you lead.

Chapter 31

Dying to Lead Characteristics

If you have read this entire book and taken the time to reflect on each chapter, you may be interested in understanding the characteristics/competencies that have been described and how they might apply to you. It may be helpful to think of the list below as characteristics as opposed to strengths, gifts, or competencies. Seeing them as competencies implies that the goal is developing strengths toward some end, while characteristics imply insight into the things that make up your character, or what you are about. While you need to be careful of over-interpreting anything out there, the following list of twenty-three characteristics of sacrificial leaders can generate honest feedback and self-reflection about your own leadership presence with others and areas for growth. This list is not meant to be used as predictors or developmental goals in leadership because that might violate the very purpose of this book. However, these characteristics highlight at least some of the ingredients found in the Bible regarding leadership, sacrifice, obedience, love, and purpose. To map these characteristics in business terms, while certainly possible, is not the point. The point is to generate an honest look at your own leadership, what you protect, and to provide mechanisms for living your faith as a leader who has surrendered his or her work for the sake of God's calling on your life.

Rate yourself on the following twenty-three characteristics and have a discerning peer or mentor rate you as well. Then consider having an honest and rich conversation about your leadership.

Directions: Read the definition of each of the 23 sacrificial leadership characteristics below and check the box indicating whether the description is like you, somewhat like you, or not like you.

Characteristic	Like Me	Somewhat Like Me	Not Like Me
Appreciative– Appreciates and rewards outstanding performance in others.			
Fair – Avoids the temptation to listen to unsubstantiated evidence and complaints without several indicators of wrongdoing.			
Impartial – Shows no favoritism to particular individuals who are friends, family, supporters, or otherwise.			
Cautious – Does not make hasty decisions but considers alternatives before responding too quickly.			
Discerning – Looks beyond outward appearance to the heart of the individual, team, or organization.			
Convicted — Knowing what you want and communicating it to others			
Self-aware – Knows how others see him or her – their strengths, limitations, and purpose.			
Irrelevant – Courageous enough to lead others and serve others, even when it is unpopular to do so.			
Empathetic – Feels what others feel and relates to their experience.			
Reluctant – Aware that the stakes are high for leaders and that he or she is responsible for the work and development of others.			

Grateful – Thankful for and to those who have made the leader's experience possible.			
Loved – Awareness of your deep need for others and your value as a human being, including a sense of being loved and accepted just as you are by God and by others.			
Connected –Aware of what is happening in the experience of others and making adjustments necessary to serve those in need. Considers whose they are as much as who they are.			
Intentional – Purposeful, slow to react unless quick reaction seems warranted. Moves with the intentionality and patience of a cat licking its paw.			
Obedient – Considers the call to obedience to God prior to the necessity for personal or organizational success. Contemplates this difficult concept.			
Sacrificial – Willing to lay everything on the line for the sake of others in your life and/or for God, even in situations where no one may become aware that you made this sacrifice. This often includes both friends and, at times, enemies.			
Confessing – Willing to say you're sorry, even to those who may have something to confess to you, but may be unwilling to say so. Aware of your imperfect nature and capacity to do wrong to others and to God.			

Authentic – The real deal. Avoids pressure to be or express something he or she is not. Aware that who he or she is also happens in relationship to others and to God.			
Complex – Understands and accepts the paradoxes in human life including things like grace and justice, freedom and obedience, hope and truth, control and empowerment, and free will and providence.			
Faithful – Full of a confidence in things he or she cannot see. Includes confidence in the face of their own increasing questions and confessions. A willingness to take risks for the sake of God's calling on their life.			
Reflective – Comfortable with silence. Deliberate in taking time to pause and reflect on their leadership, learning, gratitude, and calling.			
Learning-focused – Seeks self-improvement. Openly solicits feedback from both friends and enemies. Is not overcome by fear in the face of failure, but learns and moves forward.			
Steadfast – Difficult to shake or rattle when confronted or attacked and faces challenging situations in a predictable, settling way. Makes others feel calm because of his or her ability to stand as a rock in tough times, while also being aware of what others are thinking and feeling.			

Notes

1. Conversation with Paul Yost.
2. Viktor Frankl, *Man's Search for Meaning* (Beacon Press, 2006), 170.
3. Karl Holl quote as cited in Karl Barth, *Church Dogmatics* III (Edinburgh: T&T Clark, 1985).
4. Henri Nouwen, *In the Name of Jesus, Reflections on Christian Leadership* (New York: Crossroad, 1993), 17.
5. Ellen McGurt, "The Most Dangerous Job in Business." *Fast Company Magazine* (June 2007) [p. ?]
6. John Stott, *The Message of 1 Timothy and Titus: The life of the local church* (InterVarsity Press, 1996) [p. ?]
7. Dietrich Bonhoeffer, *The Cost of Discipleship*, trans. R. H. Fuller (New York: Macmillan, 1959), 48.